The Said

Comes From

The Seen

by JLG

VERLAG GACHNANG & SPRINGER AG
BERN – BERLIN

Jean-Luc Godard

The Future(s) of Film

Three Interviews 2000|01

Translation John O'Toole
Followed by J. A. Whistler's Ten O'Clock

At the age of 20, Ferdinand Hodler (1853 – 1918) grew a beard and so for the rest of his life, when being photographed, he was always the same person, and he liked being photographed. From then onwards he intentionally depicted the old, mature man, an artist who was already tackling his late oeuvre. His dilemma: he wanted to paint French but he thought German. He knew that, and with a beard he found expression and style.

The photographs prove it: Matisse (1869 – 1954) also enjoyed posing for photographers as a dignified elderly gentleman in his studio, who could also be perplexed that there was not always running warm water in times of war (1940 – 1944). During that time he found a biographer in the person of Aragon, who was roaming through southern France during the Occupation looking for texts and illustrations for a communist art magazine.

Back in peacetime again, renewed hardship was visited upon Matisse. The 75-year-old's eyesight deteriorated to such an extent that he was called upon to suspend painting, to lay down his brush. The late Renoir also wanted to rescue painting, and had the paintbrush tied to his fingers. Matisse resorted to scissors, coming up with a rather quirky invention, which the specialists in Paris chose to ignore for many years. What had happened? The master had his young assistants cover large sheets of papers with monochrome red, blue, yellow or greenish paint. He himself then took up the large scissors – unexpectedly, but undoubtedly a radical step in painting! In addition, the simplest of means, namely charcoal attached to the end of a long pole, allowed him to produce a physiognomic translation ‹alla prima› of a long succession of ink drawings on white paper or on a white wall.

At the same time, on the other side of the Atlantic, in the New World art metropolis of New York, a much younger Pollock (1912 – 1956) was using a smaller pole or dried up paintbrush to create his radical painterly compositions on canvas and paper.

Bizarre, bizarre, comme c'est étrange – quelle coïncidence (Louis Jouvet in ‹Quai des brumes›).

Within one year both artists surprised us: first Pollock at the Kunsthalle Basel (1958) with his ‹drippings› and large formats, then Matisse at the Kunsthalle Bern (1959) with ‹Les grandes gouaches découpés›, thirty all told. These two shows gave us food for thought, or rather discussion, for years to come. We were faced with a new pictorial space; a new concept of art was in the air. But that was also the time of Godard's ‹A bout de souffle›, another emotionally charged event.

Only a few years ago, the 2001 winner of the Nobel Prize in Literature, V.S. Naipaul (b. 1932) claimed that the novel as an innovative literary form had come to an end, for, just as creative talent burns out, every literary form also reaches the limits of what it is able to achieve. Fully aware of how much energy is harnessed by contradiction, he himself as an artist has brilliantly contradicted his own assertion: last year shortly before his 70th birthday, he published another novel provocatively titled ‹Half a Life›. To him it is the product of constant learning and hard work. Fragment of a ‹roman à clef›, or a dogmatic attitude?

Recently, after many years, I was again standing enthralled in front of the ‹Tapisserie de Bayeux›, an 11th-century piece of embroidery 70 metres long and 50 centimetres high: a story in pictures of the Norman Conquest. Vividly recounted for us contemporaries in the form of a comic. And once again I find myself agreeing with my friend, or rather the sentence she wrote a good ten years ago in my book on Bayeux: «This great tapestry never stops – no more so than all the world's battles and wars – we will keep fighting for beauty and art».

Does not the beauty of pictures following one upon the other tell the story of an entire film? Why do we need so many stories today in and around films? Why don't we simply turn back the wheels of time and return to the beginnings of cinema when films were still silent, but now with all the technical and, in the meantime, technological advances of our age. That is another proposal for rescuing images.

My stay in Normandy took me back to Godard and his visit to the ‹Atletissima› in Lausanne to look for the true face of Szabo. The Bayeux Tapestry is also reminiscent of a movie. And the place where it is presented as a racetrack with no interior. The first times around are like a visual warm-up. After a break, the visitor increases the tempo of each successive tour ultimately moving at a speed comparable to a moving picture. Experiments of this kind remain wishful thinking in museums. These days our tempo is dictated by the length of the sentences on the audiophone, which precludes contemplative viewing, or even makes it dispensable. Elsewhere the very first warm-up takes place in word and image on video. After the ‹course›, purchased cards and books confirm what has been seen, just as newspaper commentaries offer proof that there was nothing fishy about the game on the track or the playing field.

This book dedicated to Jean-Luc Godard will show how intellectual integrity can make the move from the 20th to the 21st century. Demonstration ‹par excellence› is found in his conversations, his manner and his impetus. We follow up these discourses with

Whistler's Ten O'Clock lecture as a reminder of how comparable leaps were made a hundred years ago. The book appears in the series ‹Pamphlete›.

Bern – Berlin in August 2002
The Publisher

I

For names see Glossary, p. 85ff.

11

Late January 2000. Jean-Luc Godard has just finished shooting his latest film, ‹Éloge de l'amour (In Praise of Love)›, and we hope to follow the next step, the process of editing. Our appointment is put off for two months, however, since Godard has a part in Anne-Marie Miéville's next film, which begins shooting in February.

Several weeks later, in March. In the meantime, the reason for our meeting has changed, because of the special issue of ‹Cahiers du cinéma› that is under preparation and the questions it raises. We want to ask Godard what he thinks about all the recent transformations and above all how, as both a maker and viewer of films, he is experiencing them. Godard agrees to the interview in principle. There is one condition, however, that we bring him a videocassette of Stanley Kubrick's ‹Shining›. If we forget the cassette, we can forget the interview.

Peripheria, Rolle. Peripheria is located in a vast, quiet space that comprises a library, an office and several machine rooms (editing, film recorder, etc.) The whole area is extremely neat and orderly. Godard has just completed his part in Anne-Marie Miéville's film, although the shooting schedule has another week to go. Before starting to edit ‹Éloge de l'amour›, which he hopes to wrap up in the fall, Godard also has to shoot a short film entitled ‹L'origine du XXIe siècle (The Origin of the 21st Century)›, which Gilles Jacob has commissioned for the Cannes Film Festival. The short piece is not meant as a kind of concentrated version of his ‹Histoire(s) du cinema (History/Histories of the Cinema)›. Rather, Godard prefers to organize it around two essential events that shaped the past century, psychoanalysis and history, intending to examine in what way they may lie at the heart of 21st-century cinema.

12

We pose the videocassette of ‹Shining› on his desk. We get the feeling that we are taking part in a game of poker in which one has to ante up before the other player follows. Throughout the interview, Godard readily plays along and answers our questions. At no time does the man set himself up as a prophet of the future or non-future of film. Nor does he resemble the voice from beyond the grave that is heard in the final episodes of ‹Histoire(s) du cinéma›, speaking to us from somewhere after the death of motion pictures. We discover another Godard here, one who is serene, at peace, a sharp observer of the cinema in its present state.

Any interview is more or less a game of tennis, and this is especially true with Jean-Luc Godard. The filmmaker starts off strong, acing us with a winning serve (his answer to our first question), continues with a few passing shots («I get the impression reading the critics, in ‹Cahiers› or elsewhere, that the writer could just as well have said something different, or have said the same thing about a different film»), but most often favors long volleys. Clearly, he also wanted to add to the recent debate in France that has pitted filmmakers against critics, which we had not expected. A fine, worthwhile volley, deep in the back of the court, like the rest. And the videocassette of ‹Shining›? Godard needed it to transfer an excerpt for his short film ‹L'origine du XXIe siècle›.

13

*Where is there film outside of film? What bridges link the cinema
with what is not ‹a priori› the cinema? Is the digital image still
film? Where do movie theaters, video and so on fit in nowadays?
These are some of the questions raised in this special issue that we
would like to look at with you.*

Are you really interested in these questions? When someone is the
moving spirit in a review, does he or she simply play the part of a
host, an emcee, or should we take the spirit of that expression in its
primary meaning, in the Latin sense of ‹anima›?[1] Do you really ask
yourselves these questions, or is it simply to exist, to play along, like
on television? The TV host isn't interested in what Jacques Chirac
says, and Jacques Chirac isn't interested in what the host says. It's a
mystery to me why they continue to talk about film in the newspapers, in ‹Libération›, ‹Le Monde› and so on. I'm not quite sure what
interests people. Television is not recording. Yet there is a screen, as
in film, as in the other arts for quite some time. We ought to be ask-
ing ourselves why pages are square rather than round.

To put it more simply, I would say that the cinema I was
raised in is no longer the cinema of today. The New Wave was made
up of three or four people, plus some fifteen others who later went
on to do something else. We discovered a world that nobody had told
us about. They told us not about Hitchcock or [Jacques] Becker, but
about Chateaubriand or Flaubert. That world was relatively secret. It
was a unique moment, unique, not superior. In other words, it was
one single moment. The New Wave was the only child, the only
daughters or sons of film. There was, in France especially, a critical
tradition, with [the writer, early film critic and director Louis]
Delluc and the Surrealists. The other countries had clever people,
academics, but very few critics. For [Henri] Langlois, to show films
was to make them. For Jean-Georges Auriol to publish ‹La Revue du

---

1

The French verb ‹animer› (as in animer une revue, une émission à
la télévision, to direct a review, host a television program) derives
ultimately from the Latin ‹anima›; Godard picks up on this etymology to refer to the original Latin meaning of ‹spirit›, ‹soul›.

cinéma› was the same thing. To talk about films was like making them. What I'm saying is not nostalgic, it's historical. It's very striking that nowadays you can't talk about a film without saying, «It did well,» «It didn't do well,» «It did such and such at the box office.» When Rohmer was shooting ‹Bérénice› in 16 mm black-and-white, he had twelve viewers. He wasn't thinking in terms of success or failure.

The New Wave has been greatly criticized for having emptied the movie theaters. It was made to bear the blame.

That's not entirely wrong. You'd need to go over the figures. The fascination of film was directed toward the screen, just as Douchet, even today, can be fascinated by ‹Nosferatu› or ‹Sunrise›. The fascination Anne-Marie Miéville's grandson feels for his PlayStation is not the same sort. In ‹The Sixth Sense›, something of that remains, but it's the script. The form is acceptable, but the script comes first. I'm always sensitive to, not the form, but rather the pictorial value of a certain type of projected image, which is not painting, can be in VHS or 35 mm and belongs to large-screen projection alone, although it does indeed spring from painting. People still line up for painting. I find it disgraceful to organize the shortage so that you can't see anything. If Fauvist paintings regularly circulated in towns and villages, people wouldn't go see them the way they do now. They're not going to see painting, but something they've lost which belongs to them. What are people thinking?

Shooting in video, have you ever had the feeling you were getting outside the cinema?

Never. Whether you're working with color pencils, watercolor or oil paints, it's still the same. With video I liked the personal creation, the personal essay. You can come to miss large-screen projection. Very few critics see films projected on the big screen. Three-quarters of them see films on video. And if they don't live in Paris, they haven't got the choice. If I see a John Ford on video, I get a terrible feeling. Without ‹Histoire(s) du cinéma› I would never have taken the trouble to watch these films again.

Films we hadn't seen used to be called the cinema, the invisible used to be called the cinema. Later it became an aesthetic metaphor. We loved ‹The River› because we had never seen it and Jean-Georges Auriol talked about it. There's a passage in ‹Histoire(s) du cinéma› dealing with that. There are still films that I'll never see. I can't watch more than one videocassette every six months.

Yet you must have seen quite a lot for ‹Histoire(s) du cinéma›.
Yes, because that was a commissioned piece. I wouldn't do it spontaneously. For those who came just after us, Glauber Rocha, Bertolucci, etc., the cinema was a relationship with reality, with modern Italy, for example. The New Wave was a relationship with the imaginary, taking that word as it is commonly understood. We were closer to cavemen, to the myth of the cave in any case. The relationship with reality came later, at the same time as the idea that the real imaginary requires you to proceed via reality, to put it naively: shoot out in the street, film your girlfriend, or your girlfriend's story, etc. Unknown American cinema had a much stronger relationship with reality than mainstream American cinema. [Edgar] Ulmer was closer to us than John Huston. Later on, we fell back on reality, we looked for the imaginary of that reality, and so on, both go together. Those films were never old films for us. I still don't have the feeling today that those are old films.

We never talk about old music or old books.
We've always said that about motion pictures only. Nowadays a
film that is five years old is an old film. The cinema has always
opted for the present. All that has to do with passion and doubt.
All of a sudden a continent that nobody had ever heard about appeared.

People continue to go to the movies just the same.
Yes, but it's only in Paris that you can see every type of film. I don't
know what people go to see at the movies. I don't know what the
technicians who work on my films see in movies. We don't talk
about it anymore. Once we've said, «It's good,» or «It's OK,» we drop
the subject. When Charles Bitsch was my assistant, Fritz Lang was
more than a celebrity. I talked a lot and I realized that people were
criticizing me with the excuse that I was lecturing others, whereas
I was looking more to start a discussion. I know that what I say about
a film comes from the film. I'm like a doctor talking about a patient.
The disease comes from the patient, what I have to say about it
comes from the patient, not from me first. There is something that
comes from me of course; both work together towards healing. It's
the same thing for a film, a painting or a book. You have to first see
what the film says in order to see what you can then say about it.
There are few critics today.

Would there be more films if there were more critics?
No. It looks as if I'm being nostalgic, but it's not nostalgia. People
are not interested in history, in what facts say, in what they make
them say. Balzac did a better job telling us about Napoleon than Max
Gallo, better than many historians.

2

The French preposition ‹de›, which can be translated as both ‹of›
and ‹from› in English, allows Godard to make his point simply and
gracefully, here and later in the interview, in the expression ‹parler
du film›. Something of what he means can be seen, for example, in

Why is it a mystery that daily newspapers like ‹Libération› or ‹Le Monde› continue to talk about film?

They do so in order to exist. They need to be catalogued... They have films the way others have sports. I prefer certain articles in ‹L'Équipe› on tennis matches that I've actually watched in reality or seen on television to certain film critics, because those articles tell you about the match at least: such and such a drive happened this way, etc. Film critics say what they would like us to think about a film. We might consider the evolution of Olivier Séguret in ‹Libération›. Before, he used to speak to his readers from a film, the way you can say «come from» somewhere, as opposed to speaking about something.[2] It's a little like what I wrote in a note to Pierre Braunberger, «My dear Pierre, many people have loved the cinema, but few have been loved by it. You are one of the latter.» Occasionally to criticize a technician I say to him, «You really love the cinema, but the cinema doesn't love you much.» The few articles Langlois wrote are very specific about that «speaking from,» even if you compare them with other articles written during the same period, like those by Delluc, which are very subjective. When Jean-Georges Auriol talked about Mary Duncan, the actress in ‹The River› whom he was in love with, that was new. An art critic would never have spoken well of a model, even if the painter was in love with her. The New Wave kept that extremely subjective aspect. Truffaut, on the other hand, had a particularly clear and incisive manner, that necessity to talk about films in the plural. His major article, ‹A Certain Tendency in French Cinema,› placed texts by Aurenche and Bernanos side by side. Truffaut would simply say, «Judge for yourself.» [Serge] Daney was one of the last to do that work. He described the actual thing, you'd want to go or not, in any case you'd make your judgment based on the evidence. An entire paragraph of his article on ‹L'Amant› is devoted

the dated turn of phrase «I don't know where you're coming from,» or the current clichéd admonition «Don't go there,» i.e., don't go into that subject.

to a lace-up boot. You understand what takes place in the film. Likewise, when Rivette spoke about the tracking shot in ‹Kapo›, he described it straightforwardly, like Thucydides describing the Peloponnesian War. That dimension has been lost because we no longer see the film. You tell me it's good. You'll have to show me. I don't believe you ‹a priori›. What you say is interesting. Maybe you're even more interesting than the film.

You were very subjective as a critic.

I found that I wasn't nearly as good as some others. I did a kind of temperamental criticism that allowed me to exist culturally. Truffaut was the better critic. Rohmer was more academic. ‹Le cinéma, art de l'espace› is the first text of major importance to everyone. In the cinema's heyday, American scripts were written in a way that wasn't really part of the tradition of the novel, and which allowed the producer to grasp what the picture was going to be. You wanted it to exist, not because of the idea, but because of the drama. You understood, you imagined. Nowadays three-quarters of the scripts give you nothing to imagine. Or everybody imagines something different.

Naively I thought that ‹Histoire(s) du cinéma› would spark a debate. Everyone hailed the artist's great work, but no one said that what took place between Hitler and the [German film production company] UFA did not occur as I showed it. Yet that's what interested me. I should have called those films ‹Introduction to a Genuine History Coming from the Cinema›. The two things that were the least liked in the 20th century are history and psychoanalysis, the history of everyone and the history of oneself. They are venerated yet loathed. I really like the history of others, like it too much even; I don't like my own. I am slow to come around to analysis. The relationship between these two types of history is very rarely shown. I am thinking of a text by James Agee, which I had Alain Cuny read aloud but never used, and which can be heard, although very poorly, being read by someone else in ‹For Ever Mozart›. In ‹Let Us Now Praise Famous Men›, Agee says that what really makes his blood boil is people's misunderstanding of the camera, in the broad sense of the term: a chamber for recording, etc. People think that the camera always films straight on, that they are seeing reality because they are staring at it straight on. Even a philosopher like Lévinas thinks that when you really see someone's face you could never want to kill him. The shot/reverse-shot technique is wrong. The true reverse-shot must be more or less aligned with the two figures. To hear the other person, you have to place the camera behind him so as not to see his face and hear him through the person who is listening. You find that in Welles: people move a lot, there are a lot of shadows, a lot of shots that are moving from the first frame, even in films that he didn't edit like ‹The Lady from Shanghai›.

Today's cinema is a script-oriented cinema. Since Gutenberg, the text has triumphed. There was a long struggle, marriage or liaison between painting and text. Then the text carried the day. Film is the last art in the pictorial tradition. People talk a lot about images but there is only the text nowadays. On computers, there is more text than image. It's advertising copy and commentary that dominate. I don't know what film criticism criticizes. It examines its own ideas, which it develops for the sake of a particular film's release. You have to talk about things, if not you can't distinguish King Vidor's ‹War and Peace› from Tolstoy's ‹War and Peace›. A simple fundamental language becomes a necessity: it's on the right, it's on the left, it's hot, it's cold. You have to speak coming from the film, not going to it. If you looked at all the interviews done for ‹Cahiers› over the past 50 years, you would see that initially the first person ⟨I⟩ was used far less. Film directors would say above all ⟨it⟩, ⟨this⟩, etc. Nowadays they talk about themselves, not about the film. They say, «I wanted to do that.» We'd like to hear them talk about what was done.

> When you were a critic, the cinema was part of a minority. Today it occupies a central position and is an influential force everywhere. The fine arts are interested in film, etc. The landscape has changed drastically.

Maybe, but the important thing is what people are saying about it. Take away the text and you'll see what's left. In TV nothing is left. When I watch television I watch it on mute. Without the sound you see the gestures, you see the routines of the women journalists and hosts, you see a woman who doesn't show her legs, moves her lips, does the same thing, and occasionally is interrupted by so-called on-the-scene footage. She'll be the same the next day only the text will have changed. So there should only be the text; let's do radio. The more you want change, the more it's the same thing.

Scientists are better than others because they talk among themselves about something they have in common. You can also do that with film. It's a representation of the world. If you shoot a flower, people say, «Ah, that's a flower.» There is a consensus. Several people can see it together. That thing we share ought to allow us to speak ⟨of⟩ or ⟨from⟩ and not ⟨about.⟩ The real Freudian text always speaks of, as in the Latin ⟨de⟩, ⟨de⟩ Dora, not ⟨about⟩ Dora. Jean-Georges Auriol spoke of Mary Duncan, not about Mary Duncan.

> In a way, Daney was the last in that movement. Sometimes you would get the impression that he was better than the film, that certain things came more from him than the film.

Yes, that was the end. He was aware of it. If I were to do the history of French literary criticism – literary criticism, let me be clear – there would be Diderot, Baudelaire, Malraux, Élie Faure and finally Truffaut and Daney. You could discuss with Daney, even with Jean-Louis Bory or Michel Cournot, not to mention Bazin or Truffaut. It's much more difficult today, even with honest, well-disposed people like you or Séguret. With the others, it's practically impossible. Strangely enough though, all those who say ‹I› don't want people to confuse their personal life with those times when they say ‹I›.

There's also [the question of] talent, which nobody talks about. You really offend people by saying, «What you're doing is very bad.» In private, that really hurts. But you can say that a photo has been shot poorly or well. There can be a certain consensus. With some, even among those who have helped me considerably, a dialogue was no longer possible after a certain point in time. I remember saying to Romain Goupil, «If you write that, you can't say, ‹Free Sarajevo.›»

You can of course recognize certain shortcomings. There are many of my films that I find pretty bad or pedantic. I've managed to shoot some successful sequences, but rarely films that hold up from beginning to end. Maybe ‹Germany Year 90›, ‹The Old Place›, with Anne-Marie Miéville, ‹JLG/JLG›, a few films that were never very successful.

In ‹Pierrot le fou›, there are a number of interesting moments, but the whole doesn't hold up. I've always been divided between what is commonly called the essay and what is commonly called the novel.

People used to say, «Give us ‹Pierrot le fou›.» Now that would be, «Give us ‹Contempt›.»

I've never understood why ‹Contempt› is so well liked. Commercially, it's a film that has made a lot for those who own the rights. It's always high on people's lists. I think it's simply because it comes from an American-style novel, with a basic story that is not my own. It's a film that has a number of weaknesses.

Does digital video interest you?
Of course, but I don't see any reason why we should talk about it. Why is everyone talking so much about the Internet? Why so much talk about it all of a sudden? We're left to think that digital goes with numbers, numerate, ‹numéraire›, numbered, etc.[3] I became interested in all the new media simply because there were no rules. We forget just how closed a milieu the old French cinema was, with its rules, its corporatism, as if a future writer had to join the book guild and learn how to write. There were also aesthetic rules that the New Wave thought were bad. So 16 mm and live sound recording were welcome. At the time, sound recording required an entire truck. Nagra was a great liberation. But we didn't care one way or the other. A film has to be projected and distributed according to its means. In video, there is no projection. The real image and the real text are produced. After a certain point, distribution carried the day. We were producing in order to distribute. Even the reproduction of human beings is done in order to distribute humanity in another way. The 20th century applied quite a lot but invented little, except the production of cadavers on a grand scale.

How did you shoot ‹Éloge de l'amour›?
One part in black-and-white, the other in color. If I had had lots of money, I would have liked to shoot the color portion in 70 mm, with

---

[3] ‹Digital›, in French ‹numérique›, readily suggests the idea of number, numbers, counting. Godard may also be suggesting that accounting and money hover around the word (‹numéraire› and possibly ‹numérotation›).

what was once called Showscan, which gives you a great impression of clarity. Because money was short, I chose to do the opposite, shoot in DV. In its day the New Wave would surely have used DV if it had been around. I don't see any major differences. What's important is what you do and why you're doing it. There's a bit of nonsense in all the talk about digital technology and DV. You'd have to go over the comments point by point. Nobody talks about the sound, for example, which is very bad. Moreover, at this point in time, you can't shoot without lighting; even professional video is less sensitive than 35 mm. There is something tactile in the photographic image that doesn't exist in video. The phenomenon of the cave is no more. Digital technology was not invented for production, but for distribution. Many more things can be kept in a much smaller space because you're dealing with numbers and they can be compressed. In the subway nobody likes to be compressed. In digital technology, everybody likes it. But part of the image is lost. For the sake of distribution, quality and precision are reduced. They say that the image is of ‹film quality›. It remains to be seen what quality we're talking about.

We have to admit that three-quarters of the population wouldn't want to see a film that tells their story. I like to watch people working, but a woman TV host or journalist will never watch herself working for an hour, unless out of egoism or narcissism. I can watch a worker who makes the same gesture over and over again. The worker would be bored to tears if he had to watch himself. People don't want to see their lives, only a little bit of their lives. Americans are very good from that point of view. Everything is done by the viewers, who have just enough of the springboard they need. ‹American Beauty›, which was very successful, is not bad in certain respects. If I were a film critic, that's what I would say. There is one interesting moment in the film. A young boy films his girl-friend. We see the scene in 35 mm from several angles, as well as the shot being filmed by the small camera. Suddenly we see four seconds of ‹Faces›. But if you don't show that shot, you have to do something else, what Kazan or Nicholas Ray did. Those are only samples. People like that a lot because they have the time to identify with [the sequence], then you go on to other things, come back, and so on.

Digital video also allows you to shoot with a small crew.
What is a small crew? For Americans, it's 150 people, for Claude Miller, 18. Cassavetes might have shot ‹Faces› in digital video, but the image would have been less beautiful. No one has worked as hard as I have to bring video into the pictorial tradition, and I haven't really succeeded. Certain Danish films have been successful. I like ‹Idiots›, but ‹Celebration› is merely OK.

What do you like about ‹Idiots›?
It takes its subject to the limit. In fact, that's what turned viewers off. ‹Celebration› is quite banal in its approach to family history. Certain Bergmans like ‹The Silence› are much better. ‹Idiots› is a courageous film.

One could also say that ‹Idiots› doesn't really follow the penchant toward idiocy at all since it continually maintains the idea of a separation between real and fake idiots.
You would have to act like Truffaut, take one or two sequences. You would have to act like a coach who analyzes and criticizes certain gestures. Only after that can a text that is philosophical or subjective or critical develop. You would have to provide proof. Unfortunately, film criticism doesn't really use video. For ‹Histoire(s) du

cinéma›, Bernard Eisenschitz was the only one with whom I could talk, while putting together the list of films. At least we talked about the same thing: this photo, who is this, and in what? Each of us would then offer an opinion, a recollection...

You deplore the lack of analysis.
Yes, it's the same thing that the analyst does. There's another film that we liked quite a lot, Anne-Marie and I, ‹La Pomme (The Apple)›.

By Mohsen Makhmalbaf's daughter, Samira.
Everyone said that her father helped her. I've seen one of his films, which was very mediocre, like [Jean] Delannoy's work. ‹La Pomme› is a very original film, like Cassavetes' early pictures, except that you can see it's a film shot by a young woman. How can you prove that it's good? Not an easy task. Even in seminars, that is not really done. It should be done in class, using video. I was asked to teach at Vincennes, etc. I gave them an answer, indicating the equipment I needed to be able to project several films at once. It never worked out. We were supposed to do that at the Fémis, but basically no one wanted that, not Gajos – may he rest in peace – not the professors, not the students.

How were the superimpositions done in ‹Histoire(s) du cinéma›?
It's very simple. Around the time of ‹Breathless›, I helped put an end to superimpositions in film narrative. GTC had a special department at the time. Twenty years later, someone stopped me in the street to say «You put me out of work.» I've always felt a certain debt. In George Stevens' ‹A Place in the Sun›, there are very long superimpositions. In film, the quality is not perfect because you have to make an inter-negative and you can sense a little jump when the super-

imposition ends. In video it's elementary. The two images mix like two sounds, like music. It was a lot of fun to do, and the superimposition corresponded with the metaphor of one idea taking the place of another. It's very banal.

There was a time when you used to say that in order to see, one would have to set two images side by side, as in a shot/reverse-shot sequence. We no longer have shot/reverse-shot here.
It's narrative, it's a tense. In film, too, the perfect and imperfect tenses are different. A photo of a scene from a film differs from a fixed image. The rendering is not the same. All of that was done very simply, with very old equipment. I have a studio that is not very sophisticated, neither George Lucas nor Le Fresnoy, maybe Méliès.

How did you come up with the shots in ‹Histoire(s) du cinéma›?
Initially I made a classification. I bought video tapes and I classified them. The titles came first, titles always come first in my work. I've carried around ‹Éloge de l'amour› for five years. First there was ‹Toutes les histoires (All the Stories)›, that is, all the stories that film has recounted. That first title came from a remark by Malraux, who said that in 15 years photography had recounted as much as painting had done in two thousand years. Film did the same thing. It recounted everything very rapidly. Then ‹Une histoire seule (A Story Alone)›, that is, film was indeed alone in recounting everything. Next, picking up on the word alone, ‹Seul le cinema (The Cinema Alone)›, in other words, what the cinema alone has accomplished. Then ‹Nouvelle Vague› and so on.

Once you have an outline, the rest comes together by itself. Sometimes a sequence of five minutes goes nowhere. You have to start over from scratch. Generally when you shoot a program, the text comes first, then the illustrations. It's a bit like what you do in your review, so that you're sure that it's more or less what you're talking about. If I had to make a film about the Algerian War, I'd first look for an image and only afterwards would I begin to wonder about the text. Something is given to us first, a recollection, for example. What is said comes from what is seen.

> *Let's return to digital cinema and its ‹handiness›, which you don't seem to put much faith in.*

As soon as one person is put in charge of photography, another of sound, another of direction, still another of production assistance, etc., the camera's place is determined within a certain number of set corridors, even if they are unconscious. Whether the camera has a stand or not is of no importance. Everybody says that digital video allows you to do this or that, without ever saying what was actually done. Digital video allows you to be free, but free to do what? At what moment? Actually, few things change. ‹Celebration› is a thoroughly standard, even academic film. Viewers are more or less interested in the story. It's as academic as Jane Campion's films once she began working in Hollywood. On the other hand, ‹An Angel at my Table› is not academic at all.

> *Maybe one day, films will be made without a crew, alone.*

I don't think so. It would have been done already. A man alone with his camera and people to film is [Georges Rouquier's] ‹Farrebique›. Cassavetes shot his films within his family. Certain documentary filmmakers spent an hour filming a dragonfly in the process of landing. You can't get more alone than Straub and Huillet. The result on the screen is the only thing that matters. As soon as you film four people over three months in a room, even if the crew is reduced to three people, the cost cannot be lower than two or four million francs. What is interesting about film is that it is the work of several individuals. No one has ever made films alone – maybe Warhol, Mac Laren, Michael Snow, experimental filmmakers. [Jean] Rouch had a crew of three or four people for ‹Moi, un noir (I, a Negro)›. In film, you start out with several in order to become one. That is its originality. Film is closer to soccer than skiing. People like being together with others. I do, too, what's more. On the other hand, I dislike being alone in a group even more. That situation has grown worse over time because there are fewer rules, greater fear and fewer responsibilities. Each person remains in his compartment. That's understandable inside an insurance firm, but in the framework of a film, such a compartmentalizing seems bizarre to me. Since rules no longer hold, each individual remains in his little corner. In the past, a certain number of rules were accepted, even if, in the heyday of the New Wave, we thought they were bad rules. Nowadays, when you hand around the script, or what stands for a script, nobody says a word, not even those you get along with quite well. The script is considered the bible, the filmmaker's domain, don't touch. Occasionally I say in response, «If, entirely by chance, this script described your life, would you say something?» That discussion is lacking to a large degree and that lack leads to strange relationships between people. There is a complete perversion of the notion of the ‹auteur› as the New Wave helped to develop it. At the time, the scriptwriter was thought of as the ‹auteur›, the director as someone who shot the film, an employee, which is what many great American filmmakers were, like Cukor, who was hired for his ability to direct actresses. Capra and Stevens, not to mention Chaplin, were thought of as ‹auteurs›, but in their capacity as producers or co-producers. Over the years, people came to think of Hitchcock in film like Chateaubriand in literature. Gradually it became a commonplace, so much so that I haven't had to put my name to three-quarters of my films. Currently the director of photography is thought of as the ‹auteur› of the photography. In the past there were great chief cameramen, each having a style of his own. Photography at Warner wasn't what it was at Paramount. In Italy and France as well, there were great cameramen.

I think the cinema is an image of the world. If you know how to look, you learn many things. It is a projection of the world at a given time. If we studied the way a film is made, those 30 people who come together, then part, the financial, social, sexual ties, you would see quite a lot. But no one finds that interesting. People prefer going off to study Indians. Levi-Strauss could easily have analyzed elementary family structures in Joinville or Billancourt. I believe I'm the only one to think that way and want to do that kind of work.

Do you edit your own films?

Having repeated «Cut!» over and over, I decided to do it myself. I have the time, I'm not in a hurry, I can think. For as long as possible, I'll continue to edit manually. In nonlinear editing, the image is not as good. You no longer have a photographic image. You can't wind back, the past is there by pressing a button. Time has disappeared. You can see everything you've shot. But above all I don't want to know everything I have. You know everything you have, but you don't know everything you don't have. Rossellini took me to a set where they were shooting a film by De Sica. He was sleeping and his assistant came to wake him to tell him that they had completed shot 17. So De Sica answered, «Do shot 18.» Editors do the same thing, except for the fact that they didn't make ‹Umberto D›. It's a cliché, it's better than selling tickets at Air France perhaps, but it's the same thing. The other day I was watching ‹The Lady from Shanghai› on television, which wasn't even edited by Welles; it was done by the production. Despite that, it's splendid. Is it because I still remember it from the first time I saw it, without knowing how the film was edited? I don't think so. In those days, there was a science to editing. Renoir wasn't always present in the editing room either. Nowadays it's a stereotype, they talk a lot, «We're going to do this because...» They put together an assemblage, scenes like pearls on a necklace, but no editing, no joining of two things. Moreover, these things are shot to be assembled, not edited. There is no mystery, no creation, only application. In a way, when a film is having a hard time getting made, the search for financing gives rise to much more creativity. In distribution, the routine is horrible. French cinema is doing well, even if it's in a fairly abstract way since films no longer need to be successful at the box office. They're paid for by television, which benefits and reaps financial reward from the relationship. There is no unemployment among technicians. If you wanted to shoot a film tomorrow, you would find no one. It's wonderful to be a film hand. You're kept all day long in the sort of world that is not as tiring as a factory. After two months, when you're beginning to get fed up with the sight of the people you work with, you move on to another film. It's the very image of the human cell. If you examined how a film is born and dies, you'd learn a lot about the treatment of certain diseases, cancer in particular.

You used to say that in the past about car traffic.
Yes, about Place de l'Étoile.

Can you tell when a film has been edited using virtual technology?

Not necessarily. Guiguet's ‹Les Passagers›, which I like quite a lot while ‹Cahiers› didn't really like it, and which wasn't a major success at the box office, was edited in nonlinear. Guiguet, who is of the old school in his outlook, was able to put up with nonlinear editing. I couldn't. I think I could still edit by hand, without a flat-bed editing machine, as I did with my first short film in '55 – '56. When you're editing you don't need to talk much. You sense when you have to cut.

Would you still like to shoot sports?
I find soccer a little boring. I would like to film tennis. I would have liked to film the Olympic Games. In the old days, films were regularly made about the Olympic Games. I like track-and-field events, too. I'd be thrilled to shoot track-and-field, but that would bore everyone else.

What do you find interesting in track-and-field?
You would have to show a single person, a woman, running. Television shoots that very mechanically.

In tennis, with lateral tracking shots from the back of the court,
you can see how a player moves.
Yes, but the shots are always cut. You would have to stay one game with one player, the next with the other, or one set with one, a second with the other. When you pass from one to the other, you would feel something. But people are only interested in what they say they see. Me too, when I watch tennis, I end up getting interested in the score, making an entire film in my head. In the old days, after watching Borg – McEnroe, people were completely exhausted, they put as much into it as you do when you watch

‹American Beauty› or ‹The Sixth Sense›. I'd like to shoot a film, five to six hours, on the French Open Tournament. You would see a player just as he arrives in Paris for the preliminary matches. Those players are rather poor and have to find a cheap hotel. They compete in the qualifying matches before being admitted to the more advanced eliminating rounds. I would always film the winner to be sure to make it to the finals. There you'd see what tennis is all about.

How do you see yourself with respect to the cinema overall?
Altogether on the outside.

It's become hard to follow you according to the classic logic of commercial cinema in the theaters.
Certain films have never been distributed. I can't say that I'm proud of that, but it's something I've experienced. ‹Germany Year 90› was barely seen at all in the theaters, ‹One Plus One› has never been distributed. My films can't even be presented at the ‹Cinémathèque française›, given what it's become. From that point of view, I'm not like Straub. When he complains, I tell him he's quite lucky, that there are those who are worse off than him. Then we laugh.

What kind of viewer are you? Do you see many films in the theater?
I keep up with the current cinema a little. The trailers spare you from having to see the films. Sometimes I go to see them, but it's out of weakness, a sinful pleasure. I go to see ‹Matrix›, spy films, etc. I always prefer to see a bad American film than a bad Bulgarian one. It's true in all the countries around the world. The Germans prefer to see a bad American film than a bad German one. In American

movies, there's at least a minimum balance struck between know-how and the end pursued.

There's no mistaking the merchandise.
Exactly.

There's a practical inventiveness: you learn more watching an American film than watching a French film, even as an image of the world.
Maybe, but some are awful, ‹Three Kings›, for example. I see that certain newspapers consider it a leftist film. [To Charles Tesson] You wrote a good article on Benigni's ‹Life Is Beautiful›. I don't understand why that film was so well liked, unless it's because it allows us to forget while making us believe that we are remembering. There's a good example of practical criticism. After your article, people can go on saying things but first something has to have been shown.

To continue with our review of new techniques, do you own a DVD player?
Yes, but I haven't yet managed to go beyond the control panel. I haven't managed to see a film. You need to use a remote that is too complicated. I'm in no hurry, I'll learn. Or I'll pay a maid who can handle DVD, the Internet and all the computer technology. After a certain age, you belong definitively to one period and not another. All the talk about DVDs bothers me a bit. They say you can do everything, that it's marvelous, that the quality of the image is good. If the quality of the image is bad from the start, it's not going to improve thanks to a DVD. Merchandise is no longer made to last, but to be replaced. When I began working in video, there were lots of small video studios. Nowadays there are far fewer. People made great fun of Communism. They said that America was less uniform. Nowadays

everybody wears jeans and sports shoes. I want to buy a pair of polished leather shoes and a tailored jacket in order not to do as everybody else is doing. People get things wrong the way they tell it. We have to find another term for ‹new techniques›. Video cameras are not so different from the cameras used in the past. What I like about those cameras is the small screen on the side. You need talent and dexterity to make good use of them. Sound, on the other hand, is left out in the cold in both technology and thinking about film. Critics say little about sound, unless it's in parentheses, the way they do with actors: «Sophie Marceau, extraordinary.» Extraordinary in what? They don't say. Sound is merely an illustration of the image, which is itself an illustration of something else. Given that video games represent an enormous amount of money for Sony, it's obvious that film production will be less important and of lesser and lesser quality. You can't have it all, everywhere, all the time. Half of the world's population haven't got a telephone and aren't anywhere near the point of getting one. Will it be necessarily better when they have one?

And the Internet?
I still use a typewriter.

And the screen behind us?
Part of the film recorder I use to transfer videos to film.

You wouldn't film in the street with a digital camera?
Provided that there was a film to shoot, yes. It's the same thing with traveling. If I go to Russia, it's to film something. I don't shoot film at random. I have no desire to go on the Web in order to chat with someone who lives in the Bahamas. They wouldn't be interested in what I might say and vice versa. In any case, the means are so weak

that they're not worth the trouble. We wouldn't say much, «How are you? Weather nice?»

You always suppose that there's some common interest, a stamp collection, something like that.

I have no desire whatever to communicate with a Bernard Eisenschitz over there who is interested in Samuel Fuller. There are several Godard sites, which I'm not responsible for naturally. You'll probably find information about me, most of it incorrect. I'd never dream of creating a Renoir or Einstein site. All that amounts to the same thing, people avoid talking about content. People only talk about the form, a form that is no longer form, moreover. I don't see why people are making such a fuss about it.

Yet you shot a film about telecommunications, ‹The Power of Speech›.

Yes, but there was a story by Edgar Allen Poe. Ads for the Iridium telephone used to say that you could be reached in the desert. That could never work – nobody ever goes into the desert, and those who do, go there precisely to be alone. The consequence for the cinema is a reduction of the intellectual capacity and the real life of the film. The cinema is a matter of field-work; you don't need that much technology. There are few directors today who, when they have to find a restaurant, try the dishes or attempt to find out the crew's tastes, which I find normal. There is a lot of talk and people must be very lonely and very unhappy.

So much is also being said about digital video because there could be, through technological progress, a return to a primitive cinema, a kind of return to Bazin.

I still like getting caught in the act, in the sense of getting caught red-handed. For instance, I say that I'll never use a cigarette lighter and you see me do just that on the sly. Afterwards, I can explain why I said one thing and did another. Film is a take, a certain shot. Words and etymology are important. I keep in mind the idea that the world cannot really change or improve if film does not improve. It's the place in the world where things can change. A film is like the life of a cell. You change things without harming any one, without killing or raping. Unfortunately, I get the impression that the cinema is, on the contrary, the place where the fewest changes occur. Elsewhere, there are advances made, changes, dramas, but in film there is neither catastrophe nor fantastic progress.

You don't share the point of view that digital video would be the materialization of Bazin's concept of film, because of its handiness, etc.?
Those are stock phrases.

The digital vogue, in any case, owes a great deal to that view.
It's a fake ease of operation, more intellectual than anything else, allowing you to talk around the subject, like the way people talk about the World Cup rather than unemployment. I'd say the opposite was true, that Bazin is quite attached to the photographic image. He would have written about digital film, but he wouldn't have spoken about ontology because in fact there is no digital image. An image is an image, whether it's pictorial or not, etc. There will always be a support, even if tapes disappear, even if they are replaced by cards, for example. Optics doesn't change. As long as we have eyes, optics will not change. Current lenses are not very different from those used by the Lumières. For ‹Germany Year 90›, the initial

script had Eddie Constantine as an old-style newsreel cameraman with an old camera. We made a few trials with a camera dating from 1910 that the German film library lent us. We loaded it with color film-stock, but the German lab returned it to us in black-and-white. Jean Rostand used to say, «Theories pass, the frog remains.» For now, in any case.

You get the impression that you no longer have any depth of field with digital.

Indeed. Focusing is gone, perspective is gone, everything is both blurred and sharp. There is no impression of light. It's the style of video games, PlayStation, the Internet. I prefer reading certain science-fiction novels that take place in the year 3000.

Have you seen ‹Star Wars›?

No, it's too stupid and too ugly. I went to see ‹Joan of Arc› out of historical interest. There's no talent in it. You would have to place shots from ‹Joan of Arc› side by side with other shots that you think have real talent. It is certainly true that cars have less style today than they did in the past. They're designed by computers. But because there is a need for creation, each creator adds a detail to an overall form that is the same everywhere. In the old days, that creativity was given expression everywhere. A Renault wasn't a Citroën, etc. Is that good? Is that bad? I don't know.

Sometimes cars are also given the name of a creative person, like the Picasso Citroën.

It's just a question of names. I'm very conscious of that because I realized my name was doing me harm, and I was wrongly benefiting from it. It took me some time to understand that it was working against me. I would like to present a film under a different name, although that's unrealistic.

> *Is it because of the importance of your name that ‹Histoire(s) du cinéma› has never been discussed?*

Naively I thought that it would be.

> *‹Cahiers› did discuss it, with Bernard Eisenschitz.*

Yes, that was quite good. I sent him a note.

> *You said that for once gardeners were tending to the gardening.*

Exactly.

> *You readily play with your own name: Depar-dieu, God-ard, JLG, etc.*

I wasn't the one who wanted that. For JLG, it's different, personal. Moreover, the film in question, ‹Hélas pour moi›, wasn't good. It was a professional piece of work. The most difficult thing for me in Anne-Marie's film is to keep my distance while remaining available. I'm an actor, I'm not at all involved with the direction. Unfortunately, I can't talk about film with the other actors because they don't see me as an actor. We can't talk about [Julien] Carette, Jany Holt or Kim Novak. They only see Godard offering an opinion about the cinema. That dialogue, honest, without snickering on my part, is impossible. I don't know if that kind of dialogue takes place on other films, but I doubt it.

> *Conversation is impossible while shooting your films?*

Yes, because of my name. Because of the times, too, I think.

Actors act perhaps with you and for you, but not among themselves.

I don't know.

For once, with «Éloge de l'amour», you have turned to a young actor who is fairly well known, Bruno Putzulu.

I signed him through casting. I had seen him in Guiguet's film, in which he seemed neither good nor bad, but honest. He tried to think about what he was saying. There are fewer good actors in film today because everywhere there are shows, on television and elsewhere. Political life is the same as life in the theater. Those who act are bound to have fewer flowers in their garden, as it were. Some of them, conscious of the situation, work with what's left. Putzulu seemed to me to be one of those actors. On the other hand, some lay it on thick to unconsciously overcome the situation. The same can be said about technicians and even the theater.

Do you go to the theater?

Occasionally. As I grow old I realize that it takes quite a lot of time to do things. A day can go by listening to a record or reading a book. When I go to Paris, two or three days every two weeks, I haven't got the free time to go to the movies. It's been quite some time since I've gone out to see a film.

Is it important or necessary to you to regularly see films in the theaters?

Yes, but here between Lausanne and Geneva, few films are ever shown.

You say that going to see films for you is a guilty pleasure.

Yes, like eating cake. That's already what I used to do in the old days. Unfortunately, non-stop showings have disappeared. You can't enter in the middle of a film, unless you want an insane row on your hands. I'd like to see films one and a half times, for example.

> *You worried a good deal about the filmmakers who came before you and very little, or even not at all, about those who will come after. You've even said, speaking about young filmmakers, «Let them shift for themselves.»*

What did I mean by that? I find that they talk a lot. That's what bothers me a bit. I've never been afraid of naming names, even if one isn't supposed to do that. Nowadays, you only talk about names, but when you do so to say something bad about someone, you come across as a stoolie, as they used to say. I could talk about [André] Téchiné, or Bernard Blier, who are a little younger than me. Then there is the generation that includes [Arnaud] Desplechin and [Olivier] Assayas. It seems to me that they all tell us what they're doing but don't see what they're doing. That's a bit like what I've been saying over and over since the start of this conversation. The film doesn't exist, or they are the film, but not in the sense that Flaubert said «Madame Bovary c'est moi» [I am Madame Bovary]. The cinema enables them to exist rather than their enabling the cinema to exist. Sometimes, reading the critics, I am incapable of grasping what an article is all about. If Frodon says good things about a film and Séguret bad, I have a certain idea about that film. Reading one critic is not enough. Is it the film which is like that? Or is it Séguret who, for the release of a film, says this or that? I get the impression reading the critics, in ‹Cahiers› or elsewhere, that the writer could just as well have said something completely different, or have said the same thing about a completely different film.

There is now in film an effortlessness, an easy life that fascinated Marguerite Duras. She said that there was nothing to do.

Daney said that there is nothing to see when a film is being shot.
Exactly. The day when celluloid film no longer exists, the world will have changed. A certain way of storing, of recording, that partakes of both cinema and literature, will have disappeared. The cinema provides us with a metaphor of this system. The positive is given to us; it's up to us to make the negative, as Kafka said. We would have to look up the origin of the word negative, the date when negative numbers came into use among the Arabs etc. The real history is there. But to return to French cinema today, I get the impression that it is given the positive but it is not making the negative. To be precise, it seems to me that when Desplechin made ‹La vie des morts›, he was given the positive in a very simple way, by his experience, his family, etc., and that he made the film negative, both concretely and figuratively. After that, he stopped.

Why?
I don't know. You would have to talk with him.

Would you like to have that conversation?
It seems to me that these filmmakers don't really know their film subconscious. There is a little arrogance and exaggeration in what they say. They remind me of Anelka. Cultural programs are made up of talk nowadays. Even the worst forms of justice at least have the evidence produced in court. I am also thinking of Abel Ferrara, whom I don't know very well, and the Coen brothers, whose films and comments I hate equally. You should have to say why you like something, why you don't like something, come to some kind of

agreement. This armchair is not pretty, but is good for sitting, while that one, etc. Doesn't all that come from an overabundance, not of words, but of talk? All that still depends on what nobility you attach to the word ‹talk›. In this atmosphere of ever-increasing cultural programming, films are of little importance. The environment is altogether different from what I once knew.

Do you prefer the way Hawks and Ford talked about their films, absolutely rejecting commentary?
No, that was detestable. They began to talk towards the end, like Fuller when he came to Europe. Films are the only thing that everyone can talk about and not be at a loss.

That's a quality.
Exactly. There is something naive in that, like the way they say «That's peachy» in French-speaking Switzerland. The cinema is like football. Nobody is ever shy about giving his opinion, about saying that it's fantastic or god-awful. Film is a mutant art, which comes at the end of something, is a sign of something. That's why the last episode of ‹Histoire(s) du cinema› is called ‹Les signes parmi nous (The Signs Among Us)›. Everybody can say nowadays «I'm in film.» And the press goes one further by writing, «With small digital cameras, everyone can become a filmmaker.» Well then, folks, go ahead, become filmmakers.

There is Saturday night cinema; there is no Saturday night painting. Something remains. I like to say to Anne-Marie that we'll always manage to make a little film, even if it's not seen by anyone. Rohmer is preparing to shoot a film for 60 million francs in digital and with costumes. We will always be able to make films. When I saw ‹Voyage in Italy›, I knew you could shoot a two-hour film with a couple in an automobile. I've never done that, but I've always kept it as security.

Emmanuel Burdeau and Charles Tesson interviewed Mr Godard in Rolle, Switzerland, on March 22, 2000.
First published in: ‹Cahiers du cinéma›, May 2000.

II

Five years have passed between the moment when the project entitled ‹Éloge de l'amour (In Praise of Love)› was begun and the film's
first screening at Cannes, five years during which Godard was to
write a scenario that he would eventually publish rather than film,
before shooting a film he had ‹forgotten› for a year and a half prior
to completing it. It took Godard ten years (1988 – 1998) to create his
‹Histoire(s) du cinéma› (History/Histories of the Cinema). ‹Éloge de
l'amour› is a film that goes beyond ‹Histoire(s)›, while drawing its in-
spiration from what the earlier work engendered. Godard explains
this long process in the interview below.

> ‹Éloge de l'amour› creates an expectation. Viewers look for an an-
> swer within that work to the question of how to make movies after
> ‹Histoire(s) du cinéma›. In the first part, there is a feeling of being
> set free, we're back to Paris, black-and-white photography, ‹Band of
> Outsiders›, and so on. In the second part, which is shot in color,
> ‹Histoire(s) du cinéma› is more clearly present. Do you agree?

It's video treated somewhat in the same way, but I really didn't
think about it. The sentiment of the story is more developed perhaps; it's the only conscious thing in the film that took a long time
to find its starting point.

> Why?

It's a long personal and global story, like that of the athlete who
first looks for the discipline he should run, then the stadium where
he should register and finally the race. That takes four or five years.
It's old age, too, you take more time. Memory... with Anne-Marie
[Miéville] – we often think we're losing our memories because when

we want to say a name, it's not there, we can't find it immediately, but two or three days later it shows up. So memory exists but in a different way.

What were the things you were sure about from the start and which stayed in?

The beginning goes back five or six years, the contract with Canal + dates from 1996. What especially interested me in the first phase was a story of de-chronology, and something of that was to remain, that is, a flashback. Then things began to take shape with the story of three couples. I thought that that was the one I was going to do, but I ran into problems. I realized that you can film a young person. If you or I are filmed, nobody will say first, «Here's an adult.» You need a story, you need to say what kind of adult. This is the editor-in-chief of so-and-so, this is so-and-so's lover. Whereas if you film a young person, somebody who doesn't know the situation will say, «There are three young people in an office.» No one will ever say, «There are three adults.» The same is true if it's old people. There are old people – that's the end of youth – and young people – that's the start of youth – and between the two there is all of existence. It couldn't be done, there was a missing bit, I tried... Perhaps a vague idea remained of someone who has a project and we see things from it that are rather documentary-like. I've been told that it's a documentary, but I don't know the meaning of that word.

So to come back to the order of your film...

I had a very hard time. We shot several talks or interviews with young people and old ladies in early 1999. There was a break and we shot the rest in September. Moreover, the actors hadn't been selected yet, I couldn't find them. I felt I couldn't play the role because that would have been an ‹auteur› who has a project, a film about film, something that I especially wanted to avoid. We did shooting in September, then we followed up with Brittany, which I knew had to take place, but which was very unclear to me and remained so throughout filming to some extent. It was more my past that led me to that area of Brittany, the grandparents, etc. That came from my personal history, as well as the history of the Resistance, the Occupation and the War, which began to play out like a memory for me. Which means I didn't know who was calling the shots, if it was me with respect to the film or the film with respect to me.

> ‹Éloge de l'amour› *reveals a certain logic of the flashback. The film seems to say to us* «You can't shoot a movie about love and about adults if you haven't worked out your relationship to history.» *It's as if you were saying that from now on no story is possible unless we develop a relationship to history once again.*

I agree. I wouldn't use the word ‹logic›. As soon as I use it, I feel bad because in Anne-Marie's second-to-last film I read a text by Hannah Arendt and the only thing I still recall is that she says logic is the start of totalitarianism [laughs]. So each time I utter the word I say to myself «Darn, I'm going to get yelled at.»

> *In your conversation with Youssef Ishaghpour,*[1] *you say that history is the artwork of artworks, and that film, literature and painting are subdivisions of that work of art.*

...Or multiplications. The other day, I saw written on the letterhead of our sales representative abroad, ‹A division of Canal+›. Yet in our dealings with Studio Canal, I get the impression that it's more like multiplications, that Canal Satellite is not a division of Canal+, but a multiplication. What came first historically? I would tend to say

---

[1] See ‹Archéologie du cinéma et mémoire du siècle› (Ferrago, 2000).

hypothetically that multiplication came before the other, simply because man produces offspring and multiplies, and that subsequently you have to apply something that is like division. If not, that becomes cancer or... What comes first? What comes second? I'm very concerned by these things.

We also talk about an armored division.
That's no coincidence. We don't say ‹armored multiplications›, even though armored divisions are responsible for multiple crimes.

What is especially beautiful in the film are those moments that deal with an adult age that does not exist. The young people and the old go with the construction of the film and the time sequence in the film. You announce four ages of love...
The man in the film who has a project says, «It's going to be maybe a film, an opera or a novel.» No one knows. I present him as someone who is interested in music and whose real project at first is to create a cantata about or for Simone Weil. You might think, and that is what I ended up doing in the end, that the music you hear in the film could be something from that cantata, but it's not up to me to say.

During the sequence in front of Seguin Island, I think we hear the song from [Jean Vigo's] ‹Atalante›.
Yes, that's the sound from ‹Atalante› since we were there and the barges were going by.

The adult age has fairly strong ties with the history of film and the theme of the relationship between film and television, that is, the passage from childhood art to cretinous art. What is the relation-

ship you draw between the future that is completely laid out in ‹Histoire(s) du cinéma› and what you're saying now, i.e., that people are no longer able to be adult, that there are no adults, no adult stories?

It's something that a lot of people are saying in their own way. I was reassured by the way Bruno Putzulu acted, very healthy, very upright. I hired him thinking, «He won't be putting on airs, he's honest, if he has to defend an F sharp, a B flat, a this or that, he'll defend it and do so because that's how it should be.» When all is said and done, [Putzulu's] character is what his servant says of him at the end, «He is the only person I know who tries to be an adult.» Since I didn't deal with old people... but there I'm justifying myself after the fact. It's no good if I start doing the commentary to my own film beforehand, the way all filmmakers do when interviewed... They say to you, «What were you looking to do?» and you answer, «I wanted to do this.» Some say it even beforehand and repeat it to the reporters: «I wanted to do a film against the dictatorship in Greece.» You can be sure the film is bad or mediocre. That has to be felt through the hand or the eyes if you're literary, through the ear if... That's what happened, I wasn't aware of it, but now I am, all of a sudden, I'm discovering things... The distributor, Michèle Halberstadt, said to me, «Françoise Verny's respiration» – which is her's, her way of being today – «puts me in mind of the scene at the start of the picture» – I had never thought about it – «in which a sort of homeless person says, ‹I don't know if my breath will make it until tomorrow, if my shoelaces will make it until next week.›»

Fifteen years ago, if I had thought about it beforehand while taking notes, I would have found that good. I would have tried to do it, and even if the actress didn't do it naturally, I would have tried to get her to do it. Nowadays I tell myself that it's good that it happened, but if I realize that I've decided it beforehand, I take it out. I mistrust commentary that leads to a truth. The worst kind of commentary is sports commentary. The other day I was watching the finals in tennis, Capriati versus Venus Williams. All of a sudden there was a break in the audio link with Hervé Duthu and Arnaud Boetsch, the former player, who were doing the commentary. It's already significant that the commentary is coming via other channels. It's not with the image, it's not physical. There was a Eurosport news zipper, «Please excuse etc.» Incredible! The live sound remained. Usually I watch on mute because the commentary gets on my nerves, but with tennis it's a bit of a problem because you don't hear the sound of the balls and suddenly, it was a live broadcast. It took me some time to realize it and I didn't know what to do with that freedom to enjoy the match myself, in my way, and just imagine how much I wanted to! «What a great smash! What a fine volley! Oh no, she shouldn't have done a passing shot along the line!»

I couldn't say it, like a prisoner who gets out of prison and is suddenly dazzled. It seems to me that everything is commentary today. I still prefer the old-style, run-of-the-mill commentary, the commentary on BBC animal films where you heard, «Tigers do this, etc.» But in filmmaking, everywhere except in the work of original people – I only know one or two, there are surely more – the commentary makes it impossible to have a kind of communication with the film. There is no longer the interest, unspoken at first, to wonder, «Why are they filming that? How are they filming?» because everything is written and the scenario is merely commentary on the staging in the guise of a story.

The shots done in the street make the film look a bit like an old movie because I rediscovered the taste I had in the days of the New Wave, when we filmed places that we liked or simply knew,

which we often passed through and which were off limits to filming
so to speak, according to professional cinema of the time, because
that was simply not done. Jean-Marie [Straub] does good street shots.
In ‹Sicilia› they weren't good, they were studied. In her movie, Anne-
Marie is getting down on film something of automobiles and traffic.
Here, because you feel that's what ought to be done, we're trying to
film something of the night.

> ‹Éloge de l'amour› gives us a bigger slice of life today, the homeless
> in the street, globalization and its effects, the disappearance of the
> working class, a Renault factory shot as if in a film by Murnau, a
> kind of abandoned ghost house...

Yes, but that's documentary film, it's not the same. I wanted a back-
ground, I wanted her to be living in the provinces. We looked for
locations. I saw the Renault, we said, «That's it.» I wrote the dialogue
afterwards. I remembered the title of a book by Bettelheim called
‹The Empty Fortress›. I thought to myself, Well, they also used to say
«the worker fortress,» and that was that.

> There is a gardener passing by...

They happened to be passing by when we were filming and we asked
if we could film them. Actually they are semi-handicapped people
employed by the city. At that point he says, «When I wanted to talk
to you about the CGT,[2] I actually wanted to talk about workers' strug-
gles, I wanted to talk about ‹ephemera,›» and you see a few old
ephemerae go by. You're happy because you tell yourself that at the
very moment you invent a thing, it drops by for a visit.

> The Renault episode is less nostalgic than many other things that
> you have done recently.

2

The ‹Conféderation générale du travail›, a major labor organization
in France.

I find there isn't any nostalgia whatsoever in the film. It marks a progress.

> *The shot of the Bois de Boulogne reminds me of the Straubs, of that way of showing in a site the traces of what was there before.*

It's simply the historical aspect that is being put back into fiction. Similarly, for many years I've been aware of that plaque on the Pont Neuf to the memory of policeman René Revel, who was killed – it's always bothered me that they say «Killed by the Germans.»

> *Why?*

I simply had the young woman say, «They shouldn't say that like that.» So how then? Do an issue on that.

> *Having seen your film, I stopped by the Saint-Michel fountain and I had a look at the plaque you show in ‹Éloge de l'amour›, which I had never noticed.*

No one sees it anymore. It's like street names, which are all names of left- or rightwing veterans. You don't know where you live anymore. It's that feeling. Just as he says, «Eglantine, do you realize that the project is not going to be the story of Eglantine but, to put it a bit stupidly, the story of major events which takes place through Eglantine and which is also the story of Eglantine?»

> *Does the name Eglantine have something to do with Giraudoux?*

Yes, of course. I hesitated between Clementine and Eglantine. The other day I was reading in [Serge] Daney's book maybe... I find that fundamentally he was moving more and more toward commenting on the thing, rather than on the thing itself with respect to other arts, because if you read the chronology of his texts... which means that he never approached the question via the camera, which is quite forgotten, which didn't happen to Bazin.

In other words?
He quoted a short text by Walter Benjamin from 1936 when he was writing his essay ‹The Work of Art in the Age of Mechanical Reproduction›. Daney wrote a text on that which appeared in ‹Le Monde diplomatique›. Benjamin said that people were not only going to film, but to be filmed, that people would have to get used to watching everything while being watched, and that the two great winners in that would be the dictator and the star. What more can you say? Nothing has changed.

Between the time you shot the film and the time it was edited, you let it rest for quite some time.
I was acting in Anne-Marie's film.

That's not all.
I did a short film for Cannes. And for financial reasons, the basis of all of my work, I did what I call ‹Le Moment choisi des Histoire(s) du cinéma (The Choice Moment of Histoire(s) du cinéma)›. It's a film that lasts one and half hours, containing eight ten-minute sections from the eight broadcasts, which Gaumont keeps buried, as with everything Gaumont does.

It's paradoxical that ‹Histoire(s) du cinéma› exists on an audio CD, as a book...
At the time, Gaumont refused to make the CDs, so we made them with ECM. It's funny because the CD got very good reviews. It received the Grand Prix for best album in Germany, a real review in

the ‹New York Times› by the newspaper's music critic on the film's excerpts. I was pleased. Otherwise, I was a bit pained by the reaction to ‹Histoire(s) du cinéma›. With Ishaghpour, we managed to get into the subject a little, whereas with the others, no. It was «The director wanted this or that... Magnificent! Superb!» But no one said to me, «That's not the image you should have used.» It took me ten years to make ‹Histoire(s) du cinéma›. I didn't think it would at the start. Seeing the reaction to the film, I realized I only had commentary on something that is already an historian's commentary and a bit of a filmmaker's, too. I remember something Péguy said in ‹Clio›, which is in ‹Histoire(s) du cinéma›. He says, «What would it be like if, instead of adding text to text, they added text to reality, if they added reality to reality?»

You might answer that we are not really clear on what reality is. The reference to Péguy remains very important in ‹Éloge de l'amour› and fundamentally that sort of final conjunction, the Resistance, Catholicism, history...

That's my Péguy and Bernanos side... Even though I had a Protestant education, it didn't take. Religion in Dostoevsky doesn't effect me at all. In Julien Green's work, it's more a sort of novel-like aspect that effects me, whereas for a long time I wanted to do a novel by Bernanos called ‹La Joie (Joy)›. There was a pamphleteer side to the work of both Bernanos and Péguy, or rather editorialist, since pamphleteer sounds a little 19th-centuryish. I feel that the films that must be made today, successful films... ‹La Pomme›, for example, or Anne-Marie's films, which manage to add text to text, which are no longer simply commentary... Other films comment on reality, and if they are reality, they comment on themselves. When Cézanne was painting his apple, he took an apple and he painted it, but I don't think he would have wanted to explain himself to a journalist who asked him, «Why did you choose an apple and not a pear?» Today, if we stay with film here, if you interview a director, he will explain why he chose an apple and not a pear. In fact, when he says that, he's talking about himself.

> *Instead of talking to you about the pear and the apple, we'll ask you, «Why did you put the Resistance at the center of your film?» There is a kind of reversal with respect to ‹Histoire(s) du cinéma›. It's no longer Auschwitz, but the Resistance.*

That is my story. There were events in a country that is my first and last homeland, even if legally I am considered a foreigner. I didn't know anything, I wasn't aware of anything, I felt close... I can't remember my dreams, can't relate them, and if I could recall them, I wouldn't know how to interpret them, like Freud or certain great analysts. On the other hand, when I see some of my films, I can see why I did that now. They are waking dreams. Brittany, the grandparents, the Resistance... Why? If someone came and occupied a country, what would I do? I don't know. I'm inclined to say, «If they want to come here, I'm leaving. I can try to get along, but if there is no way to, I'm leaving.» I had a film idea on the Russians called ‹Conversations with Dmitri›. Sarde and a Swiss co-producer had reached an agreement, the contracts were signed. I had booked the props, I had gone to see Max von Sydow, he agreed to the project, we sent the request to his agent, and all of sudden everything stopped. The story was to take place during a Russian occupation of France, in the final years. The Russians were coming to realize that the French were not playing along with collaboration, contrary to what they had said. They left everything for the Russians to do, empty the trash cans, build buses, make airplanes work, the metro, etc. They had appointed an old Bolshevik to the film center, one of the last representatives of 17. They chatted. Four seasons, four conversations and with the last conversation, the Russians packed up and left and the Americans landed at Deauville [laughs].

For you, when is a film completed? After shooting or editing it? When does it take on meaning?

Once it's edited. In other filmmakers' work, the meaning is there from the start and it's applied more or less successfully while leaving space for... From that point of view, I am very different from Anne-Marie. We are complete opposites. The final meaning always comes with the editing, whatever happens, whether it's editing à la Welles, when he has 250 shots in fifteen minutes at the end of ‹Touch of Evil›... or a long take at the beginning.

I get the impression that Bresson made it into the film because he passed away when you were shooting.

No, it's an old loyalty to that man and that kind of cinema, which left its mark on me, impressed me. I like his final films less, but you can't like everything. I don't think a film director, like a painter, can make more than two or three good films in 40 or 50 years. He can make a lot. I've made a lot. There are beautiful shots in some of my films, but that's all, the film is very bad. People cite ‹Band of Outsiders›, but often it's very bad. ‹Masculine/Feminine› is a bit better. There are some good ideas. Black-and-white is perhaps closer to ‹Masculine/Feminine›. After ‹Histoire(s) du cinéma›, I had to go back to black-and-white again.

Why?

Because that was what comes next in the story. The story had indeed
to take me at my word, or I had to take it at its since I had gone along
with it.

And the return to color in the second part?

If I tell the story chronologically, inevitably I am going to fall into
doing history in the anecdotal sense. So turn things around, let's
show the present first, then the past. Let's make a long digression in
the past, it's a figure the cinema invented, but it won't be a flashback. I've remained a little boy who is sincerely contradictory. Everybody would do the present in color and the past in black-and-white,
let's do the opposite.

> *The break is very clearly marked. The very first shots give the im-*
> *pression of a color that is slightly doctored. We go from a New*
> *Wave realism to a color that is bit synthetic.*

When we did that, we called it the ⟨Fauves⟩, with degrees of color
that were more or less saturated. It's true that my taste in painting
is for the Impressionists, from Turner to Kandinsky, the German
School, in other words, the Fauves.

> *You certainly chose Brasillach for a precise reason, because he be-*
> *comes an intense presence.*

Indeed, it is Brasillach. Those are terrifying things he wrote, but I
can't forget that it's also Bardèche's and Brasillach's film histories,
both of whom were ⟨normaliens⟩.[3] You have to link them up to the
history of the New Wave one way or another. That text was quite
powerful.

> *In the end, it is Brasillach as if it were Aragon sung by Leo Ferré.*
> *There is something surprising in that inverting of roles.*

---

[3] That is, graduated from the prestigious École ⟨normale⟩ supérieure;
⟨normalien⟩ is the equivalent of ⟨Ivy Leaguer⟩ in the United States.

Yes, but it's only the text that counts, it hardly matters. You situate it historically by saying that it's someone who was executed by firing squad after the Liberation of France...

...for what he wrote.

For his acts, his acts of writing. I wanted people to hear «Liberation of France;» likewise, if it's Bataille's ‹Bleu du ciel› that's being talked about, I wanted it said that the text came out during the Liberation of France and that it drew 200 readers.

Before it was Malraux and ‹L'Espoir›, and here it's Bataille...

Really, we can't always say nice things about Malraux [laughs].

There is a simplification of America that is increasingly obvious in your work. When America appears, it is only as a third-rate cook slinging hash, whereas Jack Palance in ‹Contempt› wasn't that.

He was a poet.

There's something like a decline of America's image.

No, it's purely the politicians. If instead of that representative we called Spielberg's assistant, you could put François Hollande or Lionel Jospin, it's the same thing, politicians. As the grandmother says, quoting Cioran, «We are all practical jokers, we survive our problems.» Everybody talks about Americans, but they don't have a name. A Texan from Texas is called a Texan, a Californian from California likewise, and so on. But the United States doesn't have a name.

We are the country memory comes from. The idea of the American or person from the United States who comes to steal memory...

That wasn't intentional, that's unconscious. How can we explain that they want it? The Russians didn't want to invade, they wanted to dominate, and so to dominate they invaded everything they could. That's what ‹Conversations with Dmitri› was about. What interest was there in coming to occupy Paris? When the Czar came, after Napoleon, he was bored and wasn't keen on staying. How is it that the United States wants to be the world's conscience... You only have to look at their films, between the United States and Germany. Who has made the most movies about the Second World War? The United States. Eighty percent of the time those are films with Germans. How many American actors were happy to play Germans? When Fuller shoots ‹The Steel Helmet›, those who are so fond of the shot/reverse-shot don't even do the reverse-shot from the Korean side. With Vietnam, we don't see North Vietnam. We see a little of South Vietnam, but for Coppola or Kubrick, the Vietnamese are ‹gooks›. It's odd, they could do something else, but they've run out of ideas. American film in the 1930s hadn't run out of ideas at all, not until the 1960s. It was a driving force, then it was transformed into television. America is especially on during off-peak hours, in other words, eighty percent of the day... It's like in tennis. They say you have to win the crucial points, but if you win only the crucial points, you lose the match. America has won the match as far as television goes, thanks to off-peak hours.

It is odd all the same that Europe and the whole world sees practically the same images all the time. In French, unlike other languages, the terms are interesting. In France they say production, distribution and after that exploitation.[4] TV is immediate exploitation, and broadcasting. Nowadays, a good film is produced but then it isn't distributed or broadcast. That's why it doesn't work. There are exceptions. With works of art and objects, it would be better to say

---

[4] ‹Exploitation› in French can mean both taking unfair advantage of, and putting something to good use, developing it and making a profit from it. Here Mr Godard means the latter.

«It's distribution.» A television series isn't produced, it's produced for distribution. Here production is an annex of distribution. In film, there is still – while shooting the picture especially, and if later you can do the editing – an aspect of the production that is like a mother who produces a child. I've never had a child, so the people I talk about it with tell me, «You're not qualified, you never had any,» and I say, «Six out of seven days, no, but one day out of seven it ought to interest you to talk with me about it because I didn't have any,» trying to be honest and intelligent with regard to myself. My point of view is, the papa doesn't do anything. He has confidence in his lady and the mama produces. He's sent something, so he doesn't even know if it's him... That's the story Dolto used to tell about Joseph and Mary. You don't know and therefore if you're not a good Joseph, you need to start over again... Afterwards, it's the attach-ment of the child who needs the father or the role played by the father.

In ‹Histoire(s) du cinéma›, you say that America is ‹a girl and a gun›. It was Griffith who said that, not me. What he meant to say at the time was fairly simple. You only need a revolver and a girl and you can make a film. Likewise, when I saw ‹Voyage in Italy› I thought, «With two characters in a car you can make a film.» If you want to, it can be done. Lelouch did it. That doesn't mean it will be a good film. But at the time, I remember it was reassuring to be able to say to myself, «Whatever happens, I will be able to, even if it's with a pencil and drawing paper. It won't be with a camera and film, but it won't be a novel either. It will be a film.» To make films, you need a minimum of money, even if you set out today – which people don't do – to shoot a short video, you need a little minimum. It costs some-thing and you have to regularly earn more than 10 000 francs per

<hr>

5

‹Blanc› in French means both white and blank; a ‹white book› (livre blanc) is a special report issued following an official inquiry. The ‹black book› that is mentioned refers to a recent publication in France on the crimes of various communist regimes, ‹Le Livre noir

month. There is a financial effort that I appreciate in the camera's function, it's close to life. You have to earn your keep, you have to earn your film in the same way.

At the start of the film, we see the book with its white pages. There is no text inside.

Exactly, in Putzulu's hands. It's the metaphor of the white book.[5] People even talk about the black book, the black book of Communism...

In the first part, the white book is, in this case, the blank page.

I didn't want people to think of the blank page but I couldn't avoid it, each person makes his interpretation. When there is some business that's not clear, a commission is held and eventually they publish what is called a white book. It's the film's white book. We could go on, it's like white bread, there's plenty of it [laughs].

In this instance it is you who are doing the commentary, because someone watching the film sees a blank page.

In our day and age, you see a book and you think ‹page› because you are a writer. On the other hand, I thought, «Since we see a book, let's hope that people don't think of the famous blank page right away.» If I had wanted people to think of a blank page, I would have chosen a blank page. I didn't want to because that would have been read as «project for a film that isn't going to be made,» etc. Here it's an historic document. The white book belongs to history, it's historians who produce white books on the Gestapo...

That's precisely the point, they're never white, they're black. In the film, Tristan and Perceval are both names that have come down to us from history and the names of networks.

du communisme. Crimes, terreur, répression›, by Stéphane Courtois et al. (Éditions Robert Laffont). The discussion centers on the interpretation of the white, or blank, pages of a book seen at the start of the film.

Exactly, it's poetry. I wanted to allude to courtly love... It's not apparent in Rivette's ‹Joan the Maid› because it's not what interested him. It's a film I like very much. It occurs to me that the two films by Rivette that I like are costume pictures, ‹La Religieuse (The Nun)› and ‹Joan the Maid›. Why? England occupied half of France at the time and courtly love began at the court of the English king, so there's something about the origin that I'm trying to get out haltingly. I did indeed invent the name of the network, Tristan and Iseult. I remember quite clearly before going to Brittany, Sarde, the producer, said to me, «How is it going?» And I said to him, «OK, we've begun shooting.» «Shooting what though?» I said to him, «Well, nothing. We can't see anything, but I have faith, hope...» There's a phrase by Denis de Rougemont in ‹Penser avec les mains› (to think with the hands) that I still know by heart. I quoted it in ‹Histoire(s) du cinéma›: «It is in hope that we are saved, but that hope is real for time destroys the act, but the act is the arbiter of time.» If I were speaking as a film critic, if I were doing the film's critique, I would say that this picture tried to film acts that time destroys, but time in turn will be judged by those acts.

> The act is arbiter of time, but what is going on at each moment of the film... the film as a totality?

I might say, if it's not too pretentious: to have that feeling of act and time, two things that go together. In the end, it's like quantum mechanics at the turn of the century – when they discovered that, all they could say was, «We don't know the speed of the particle but we do know the area where it is, and if we know the area where it is, on the contrary we don't know its speed.» So there is a double relationship of act and time, which a scientist cannot express like that.

63

Aren't there two speeds in the end? There is the movement of the particles, a kind of freedom, and at the same time there is a restrained speed. Despite everything, a scenario is applied...

All the films that I find worthwhile end up with a scenario, just as Malraux said, «Death transforms life into destiny.» Every bad film begins with a scenario and ends with a copy of the scenario. You can see it quite clearly in numerous French films. In many of them, thanks to youth or originality, things are tried but they can't bring it off. After 40 minutes or an hour, they ought to stop, but they depend on the scenario which states that Paul has to go and kill so-and-so and they film it. They've left behind the film they had started at the outset.

We could also turn that logic on its head, i.e., this film shows that the film only comes together at the end. These are scenarios that are made to show that scenarios aren't needed.

But even films like Visconti's, for example, which are very elaborate, obey that – we need to find a better word than ‹logic› [laughs] – obey that necessary freedom, even if they are put together extremely well, are intentional, closer to theater in that respect. Such was my taste.

All the same, that's at quite a remove from your cinema.

Yes, nevertheless I'm quite drawn to that, but I'd never know how to do it because I can't see what I would have people do. I would very much like to write texts for the stage. I like writing dialogue, but what would I begin with? Whereas for my films, I've always felt that there was a gift, that you received something and afterwards you could... It's closer to painting. You see a tree leaf and you say, «I'm going to draw it.» You can't be entirely alone, it's too much. There has to be a small group, there has to be the need for a vision. I'd like to make a film with a real reverse-shot. There has never been one. There has only been what the Americans did, but that has become any- and everything. All the great films known until now don't have shot/reverse-shot – for one reason: we don't know what a real reverse-shot is. Lévinas often has good ideas, but when he talks about the gaze of the other that cannot be killed, the other who is such that he can't be killed, he is doing a bad reverse-shot. Film can touch on such questions perhaps. I can't because I don't have Lévinas's intellectual capacity, but if we were working together, we'd manage to come up with a phrase that is deeper, worked out with greater care, in that domain only. As it happens, I have a project for a short film on lovers meeting in the various ‹arrondissements›. I proposed something. I have no idea whether it will ever be made. I'd call it ‹Champ contre champ (Shot/Reverse-Shot)›. It features a girl called Adrienne Champ and a boy called Ludovic Champ.

Otherness is a break. It also depends on language...
That way of doing what is called shot/reverse-shot nowadays came in with sound. Now TV uses and abuses it everyday.

Jacques Rancière and Charles Tesson interviewed Mr Godard on April 4, 2001.
First published in: ‹Cahiers du cinéma›, May 2001.

III

At 71 Jean-Luc Godard possesses a combative spirit that is truly unique, a way of seeing things that is more sensitive than most, and a rare capacity for indignation.

Godard has been a passionate sports fan all his life. Just before presenting his latest film (‹In Praise of Love›) at the Cannes Film Festival, the filmmaker agreed to examine the changes affecting an activity that the media – as he sees it – are no longer able to capture and convey.

You and sports go back many years, don't you?
I played a lot of sports when I was young. I played sports ‹naturally› and didn't see any difference between running, soccer or skiing. I liked playing everything. Tennis goes back even further. I must have got that from my mother. Even as a child I used to read write-ups in ‹Illustration›. Later, I settled in Paris. I signed up for basketball at the Stade Français, but I quickly realized that it was another world, that if you really wanted to excel, you had to do only that. So I dropped it... Then, about fifteen years ago, I took up sports again, as a pastime, for my health. I started playing tennis again, the way I might do a workout. With that I started ‹watching› tennis more closely. I was very interested in McEnroe and Mecir. I also liked Jim Courier. How could they criticize him for reading a book between sets? Sampras is good but I prefer Pancho Gonzales. I also keep up with cycling, a little bit less with soccer, and track-and-field. But I don't care for Formula One.

Why?

Too many headaches associated with it. Paradoxically, people like automobiles and complain about traffic jams! If you like one, you have to like the other. Since I don't like traffic jams, I don't like cars that much. And if Alain Prost likes cars, I can't like him. Then there are all those guys covered with advertising from head to foot shaking their bottles of champagne. I find that vulgar. The ceremonies around the podium are indistinguishable from the ceremonies around the Golden Calf. And then there is the CO_2 and Bush Junior...

Even someone like Senna doesn't make the grade in your eyes?
Oh, you know, in terms of racing cars I haven't gone beyond Fangio. I used to be a real fan of the Sommer-Wimille duels, the old, authentic Thousand Miles. That is a world that has disappeared, a world that was spread by word of mouth, a world that was listened to on the radio... A little later I became a soccer fan for a while. You might say that if Communism ever truly existed, it was the Honved team from Budapest that best embodied it. I clearly remember Puskas the Galloping Major, Golden-haired Kocsis, Czibor the Mad Winger, and the Deputy [Hidegkuti]. I have never seen any other team that knew how to play together so well. It's true that a lot of goals were made against them, but they always scored more than the others. I saw a documentary on Puskas. He would go out to do his shopping while juggling the ball [Godard stands and imitates the player]; he'd buy his newspaper with the ball on his foot, go to the butcher's and the ball was still on his foot.

Do you read sports news?
Yes. ‹Sports› with its blue wrap, then ‹Élan› with its yellow one, and ‹L'Équipe› with its red one, which merged with ‹Élan›. I still read ‹L'Équipe› a little. It's the only French daily that hasn't changed too

much, that doesn't lie. I really find out in their write-ups what happened the night before. I also find the enthusiasm that sets sports journalism apart from the other kinds. I used to like Jacques Goddet's articles, their lyricism, their naiveté, and especially their prose style. Like me, the head of ‹L'Équipe› must have learned in composition class that you're not supposed to repeat yourself. Instead of writing a second time ‹Anquetil›, he would write ‹the Hutchinson-Helyett-Leroux pony› or ‹the youngster from Quincampoix›. It's second-rate Victor Hugo but it fits in well with sports. I also liked Gaston Meyer's articles, very technical. It was like André Bazin at ‹Cahiers du cinéma›. He was good at explaining things, in a way that was very clearly argued.

How do you experience sports today?

I don't watch much television but I still watch sports, because there's something there still in which the body, again, doesn't ‹lie›. The champions can be rolling in money, filmed horribly, yet they are still themselves. Sotomayor can't say «I jumped 2.31» when he only jumped 2.30 meters. It's impossible. Nobody would believe him. Even [Bernard] Tapie, when he lost in a soccer stadium, couldn't say «I won,» whereas in other fields, even as a government minister, he could say whatever he liked. Politics, movies and literature lie, not sports.

Except with doping....

That's the ‹Mafia› side of sports. There are all those interests at stake, all those directors, all those big suits. But beyond that world of software and money, or in spite of that world, a certain ‹truth› remains. That's probably why sports are so enjoyable. They hold out that hope still.

Is it because fiction films are unable to capture that ‹truth› that they are so poor at accommodating sports?

Fiction can <u>recount</u> something but it cannot <u>account</u> for something, it can tell a tale, but it can't render an account. You would have to shoot not only the champion and the match, but also the evening before, the evening after, the girlfriend, the family... You would have to have films that ran fifteen hours. Who's in favor of that, apart from Andy Warhol and me? The only sport that is getting by somewhat is cycling, during the Tour de France, where they're forced to ‹render› time as it elapses, or the Liège – Bastogne – Liège race, because of the ‹Fauvist› violence of the Vlaminck landscapes there. Shooting sports amounts to showing the work of the body without interruption. The problem is that that priority has disappeared. The way of ‹showing› things has totally deteriorated.

Even on television?

Especially on television! TV no longer respects the thing being filmed. It's just a matter of programming and broadcasting. It's amazing how things have changed! Between the Sydney Games and those of 15 or 20 years ago, the differences are enormous. I liked how certain cameramen used to focus on women high jumpers. They'd spend 15, 20 seconds on a swinging arm, a bowed head [Godard mimes what he means]. They wouldn't hesitate to shoot the jump before the jump. That's all over today. Everything is accelerated. It's the jump and nothing else. Above all no waiting, and no patience...

Because time is of the essence, because you have to move on to something else?

Because they're bored. As soon as they're off in the distance, cameramen grow bored, so they zoom in and get close. As soon as they're in close, they grow bored again, so they zoom out and back off. My worst enemy is Françoise Boulin, the director in charge of the French Open! She's in her studio in front of 12 screens, which she didn't even have to go out and buy herself, and she juggles this and that and zaps from this to that. How are you supposed to ‹see› in front of 12 screens? You don't see an image, you ‹scramble› it. And then there is the commentary.

The commentary?
The whole problem starts right there. Imagine if we heard the voice of Jean-Paul Loth coming out of speakers scattered around the stadium during the volleys at the French Open. The TV viewer puts up with what the stadium audience would never put up with because the image of the game is so lacking, they have to lend it a semblance of being present. It has to be ‹doped up›. The commentary, which replaces real time, celebrates the demise of the body working. The body is the image, as silent as the grave. The commentator is the desecrator. He hinders us from experiencing our freedom as viewers, which is already constrained.

How would you show things?
[Godard hesitates] I'd choose an average guy arriving from Pakistan or South America who is going to play in the qualifying rounds. He's in Paris. He doesn't have too much in the way of money, looks for a cheap hotel. He takes the metro, plays. Then he's beaten. With the following round I'd focus on the player who had won, then on the winner of that match, which would necessarily lead us to the finals. What is truly disappointing today is that the matches are filmed the same way, the first round just like the last. It's the reign of the always identical. It's annoying to see the same shots constantly, the

player waiting, the player serving. For someone interested in the game like me, I'd like to see how all that sorcery is prepared and played out. Rather than forcing me to shift over to the other side of the net, I'd prefer to remain with one player a little. In all sports, TV viewers are forced to ‹follow›, they have no choice. Sometimes they show us ping-pong, but never kayaking or rock climbing. I can't think of a solution, but I would like once to see just one player, filmed a bit like the way Stendhal shows us Fabrice at Waterloo: he doesn't know where he is, or knows very little in any case. With swimming it's the same thing. They don't know how to deal with it. They've come up with nothing new since Jean Vigo's documentary on Jean Taris [‹La Natation›, 1931]. There is less and less of a difference between the commercials and the reruns, the presentations and the live broadcasts. Everything is beginning to look alike. Cloning is already with us.

Is there too wide a gap between reality and its representation?
[Excitedly] When you go to a track-and-field competition, you can easily see that you see very little! Not long ago I went to a competition in Lausanne because I wanted to see Gabriela Szabo. I wanted to see how a little mouse winds her way along the track. I barely saw her, but I was glad to be aware of that. My recollection, even partial, is much more powerful than all that I had seen of her on TV. The same goes for Anna Kurnikova. When I saw her at the French Open, I was amazed. On TV I took her for an average Russian, fairly broad-shouldered, with a face like Boris Yeltsin's, when in fact she's really pretty, really elegant. On TV Thomas Muster is a hulk, whereas seen in person he's a savage wolf, lanky and slightly bewildered. Television films the star and his glory, not man and his misery.

Are TV viewers being lied to?
In terms of speed, for example. A shot by Venus Williams has nothing in common with one by Hingis. Yet television is incapable of showing that. And so they forget the essential, they forget the bodies. They get people's minds all worked up but true spirit is missing.

You've had several sports projects in the works, but you've never seen them through to production. Why?
Because things didn't work out. I was supposed to shoot a picture about the Los Angeles Games in 1984 with Coppola, but the talks came to nothing. I was also in discussions with Canal+ but they backed out.

What would you say to young people who prefer watching sports on TV rather than in the stadium?
That that's their business... Maybe they prefer traffic jams, too... And I'm sure the beggars prefer ‹Titanic› while ‹Du soleil pour les gueux› (sunshine for the beggars) sank at the box office.[1]

They do have one argument: thanks to slow-motion or VHS, television allows you to watch the action over, to understand better.
To study, maybe, supposing that the film was shot well enough in the first place. But if you've been to a show, why watch it over again? The emotion won't be the same. On the contrary, you should be happy not to ‹see› everything, to keep part of the mystery, in order to dream. Even in the theater, depending on whether you're in the second or last row, you don't see the same thing. It's only at the movies that everybody sees more or less the same thing. They darkened the theaters and widened the screen for that, so that everybody is on an equal footing. That was projection's strength, which is

---

1

A film by A. Giraudie. Godard plays off the title of Giraudie's film in the first half of this sentence, speaking of ‹gueux› (beggars, tramps, scamps) flocking to see James Cameron's hit film about one famous ocean liner's unfortunate run-in with a wayward bit of polar ice.

precisely what television killed. Projection has disappeared on television, hence the ‹project› has disappeared. Now there is only broadcasting, diffusion, that is, something diffuse. Furthermore, on TV they only shoot the nobles, the winners, at the expense of the commoners and the losers. You never see a Fourth Division soccer game on TV or juniors tennis tournaments.

It's excellence that counts...
I don't know. People have the courage to live their lives, but rarely to imagine them. I'd like to watch the weakest, the most inexperienced, to learn something thanks to them, to be close to them. With soccer it's the same thing, they're happy to film the outcome, the spectacular. For me each game is different. Auxerre – Sedan is not the same thing as Moscow's Dynamo against Turin's Juventus! It's not the same story and therefore shouldn't be shot in the same way. The players end up having the same reactions, the same expressions of hatred in winning as the Hutus had in exterminating the Tutsis!

Is it possible to watch sports without taking sides?
It's hard. You're for one and not the other. It's completely arbitrary for me. Granted, I'm for the Russians, against the Americans. But I couldn't really explain why. Because of Russia's woes maybe? In general, I'm usually against the favorite.

Isn't there a paradox here inasmuch as we have a harder time ‹seeing› sports, whereas directors are using more and more close-up cameras, slow-motion techniques, etc.?
They're not looking for the truth of things, they're looking for the glory of the event. They want to bowl viewers over. They inhabit the

camera, take it over like squatters, but the spirit of the camera doesn't inhabit them, nor does sport.

Maybe sport can't be filmed?
That's probably the case... Dance is hard to film, singing too. And that's fortunate.

Is Leni Riefenstahl's version of the 1936 Berlin Games, ‹The Triumph of the Will›, a good sports film?
It's a woman's point of view. She had considerable financial backing and new techniques. She shot a little more ‹at length›. It's not as phenomenal as people have said, but to a degree it's very good.

In that film, commentary often takes precedence over aesthetics unfortunately...
Riefenstahl had a bias linked to Nazi ideas. Yet strangely enough, that bias is much less fascist than what they're forcing on us nowadays in my opinion.

Why?
In Riefenstahl's work there was, for all that, great respect for the thing filmed. There was a science to framing the shot. Nowadays we are buried beneath an avalanche of filmed images. Anybody can call himself a cameraman and think he's framing a shot. In the past you had a Kodak box camera and you shot two or three photos. There was great humility with respect to ‹that›. Nowadays there is no longer any difference between someone who owns a camcorder and a Stanley Kubrick. Now it's up to the viewer to distinguish the two. Granted he has to have a minimum of critical judgment!

Along the same lines, Zidane, McEnroe, [pop star Johnny] Hallyday, [actor Alain] Delon, aren't they one and the same thing?

McEnroe and Delon, maybe there's something there. Still, I don't know if the comparison is called for. One kind of wonders...

You say «everything is too tied up with money.» Yet when movies were the province of the big studios, when the freedom to create was restricted, films weren't necessarily bad....

Because studio bosses in the US were poets of money all the same, whereas modern sports are not owned by big studios, they are owned by industrialists. At the head of the great studios were entrepreneurs, who had taste, I don't know, but who had character in any case. Individuals who loved the movies. I don't know whether sports bosses love sports... The champions are also very much responsible for the situation. It's a very conservative milieu, very conventional, very ‹normal› in the end. Coppi and Van Steenbergen were genuine personalities. Borotra was a personality. A Micheline Ostermeyer is impossible nowadays: a champion who wins medals and plays Chopin! The year Marcel Bernard won the French Open, he was working at the French foreign office... Now there is this notion of the record that trumps everything else, to be the best, the first [Godard snaps his fingers several times]. Those are really schoolboys' ideas that ought to be analyzed.

But doesn't the fact that Beamon did 8.9 meters [in Mexico] make his jump even more beautiful?

Probably. Performance is part of sports. It's performance that encourages those endless ‹feats of magic›. Perhaps Rilke came up with that formula of his while watching a record being set: «Beauty is the beginning of the terror that we are guilty of enduring.» What bothers me is the exploitation that comes afterwards, the ‹show› that goes along with it. Nowadays you see the champions raising their fists, showing their teeth as soon as they win [Godard imitates what he means]. It's awful. Even women are getting into the act now.

The frenzy of winning...

Poor Pasteur.[2] Excitement, sure, but the frenzy of winning – that's for [General Jacques] Massu in Algeria, that's for war. It's a far cry from sports. Even ‹Goofy› Knerten thinks it's OK to do that. Why does he go down to that level? Because he saw it on TV, because he feels he ought to... Off by himself he wouldn't have done that. The trend is awful.

Do champions lack personality?

It's funny because more and more the grand personalities are looking to ‹depersonalize› themselves. Like movie stars, champions are shutting themselves up in their shells, living in their own closed world. If I were the owner of Paris-Saint-Germain, I'd make sure that Anelka's contract stipulated that he be filmed at home eating breakfast, chatting with his girlfriend. You'd get two percent in the ratings, no one would be interested and people would leave him alone.

Yes, but in filming that you would also run the risk of demystifying the personality.

Why fear demystifying when mystery no longer exists? In any case, at 200 million [old French francs] per month, Anelka is a personality out of my range...

Anelka isn't responsible for the money he's paid...

[Godard cuts him off] We're always responsible for our acts! Anelka could play soccer for his own satisfaction. No one is twisting his arm

---

2

In the original Godard cleverly plays off the interviewer's initial remark, «La rage de la victoire...» (the frenzy, madness, ‹rage› of the victory). ‹Rage› also means rabies in French; hence Godard's reference to Louis Pasteur.

to sign with Real in Madrid. Having done that he can't demand to be free as well! If I sign a contract with Catherine Deneuve or Sharon Stone, I have a whole army of lawyers and agents on my back. I can't do a thing. When I sign Delon, it's a little better because there is a certain level of candor; a handshake is as good as a contract.

Speaking of the last World Cup, you were heard to say, «If they had known that the whole thing would end up with Barthez embracing a McDonald's hamburger, they would have kept up their guard.» Was that resentment, anger?

I really found it disgusting. Frankly he didn't have to do that. Barthez is a good goalkeeper. He played well, gave us a beautiful show. Let's just say he doesn't see what he's done, isn't aware. It's true he doesn't have as much style as René Vigual.

What about Marie-José Pérec's attitude in Sydney?

It was kind of nice what happened to her... It's proof that the girl is not ‹normal›, that is, she doesn't belong to the norm. I was glad she went to Rostock [in the former East Germany], in that hole with that weird Doctor Mabuse. I really liked that «East Germany, the bearer of all the sins of the world» aspect. I know Rostock. I filmed a fine woman runner there, Krabbe. I needed a girl jogging, she was already involved in a suit and she needed a friend (and money).

Like actors, athletes have got to live, but the decline is painful of course.

The decline of the glory, yes, but nobody dies from that. I saw Borortra win the French Indoor Championship at 50. They were playing on flooring and the ball was faster than at Wimbledon. It's easier for actors. There's always ‹Lorenzaccio› or ‹King Lear›, the repertory. What is true is that even in movies old age is accepted less and less. Gabin and Simon aged better than Belmondo or Delon today. Athletes come to resemble actors in having a hard time accepting the moment when the bravos stop coming, when the ‹dream› comes to an end. My one and only dream is to compete at the French Open dressed in an overcoat, sporting heavy shoes and smoking, and maybe reading this text by Fréderic Prokosh on Bill Tilden entitled ‹Une Sarah Bernhardt›: «Well, let me tell you something, my boy. Tennis is more than a simple sport. It is an art, like ballet. Or like a stage play. That moment I enter the court I feel like Anna Pavlova. Or Adelina Patti. Or even Sarah Bernhardt. I see the footlights in front of me. I hear the crowd whispering. I feel a cold shiver. Win or die! It's now or never! It's my life's crucial moment. But I'm old, my boy, old. My legs are giving out on me. Will the last act be tragic?»

Your dream is to compete at the French Open – and win?
Obviously!

Jérome Bureau and Bennoît Heimermann interviewed Mr Godard early in May 2001.
First published in ‹L'Équipe›, May 9, 2001.

81

Jean-Luc Godard

The Swiss director, screenwriter, editor and actor, was born in Paris in 1930. In the 1950s, together with Jacques Rivette, Eric Rohmer and François Truffaut, Godard was one of the film critics who chose ‹Cahiers du Cinéma› as the organ for their philosophy that the director of a film should also be its author. His film ‹À bout de souffle› (Breathless) marks the beginning of the French New Wave, which revolutionized the art of the motion picture, freeing the medium from the shackles of its long-accepted cinematic language by rewriting the rules of narrative, continuity, sound, and camerawork.

Godard was married to actress Anna Karina and subsequently to Anne Wiazemsky; today he lives and works with Anne-Marie Miéville in Rolle on Lake Geneva (Switzerland).

Selected Filmography

_____1959 À bout de souffle (Breathless)
with Jean Seberg and Jean-Paul Belmondo
_____1963 Le mépris (Contempt)
with Brigitte Bardot, Michel Piccoli, Fritz Lang and Jack Palance
_____1964 Bande à part (Band Of Outsiders)
with Anna Karina, Claude Brasseur and Samy Frey
_____1965 Pierrot le fou (Crazy Pete)
with Anna Karina and Jean-Paul Belmondo
_____1966 Masculin Féminin (Masculine Feminine)
with Jean-Pierre Léaud and Chantal Goya

_____ 1968 One + one (Sympathy For The Devil)
with Anne Wiazemsky, the Rolling Stones and Black Panthers
_____ 1988 Puissance de la parole (The Power of Speech)
Video-film for Telecom
_____ 1988 Histoire(s) du cinéma
the first two chapters of his eight part television series
_____ 1991 Allemagne année 90 neuf zéro (Germany Year 90)
with Eddie Constantine
_____ 1991 Hélas pour moi (Oh, Woe Is Me)
with Gérard Depardieu
_____ 1995 JLG / JLG
Autoportrait de décembre (Self-Portrait in December)
_____ 1996 For Ever Mozart
with Frédéric Pierrot and Madeleine Assas
_____ 1998 The Old Place
the remaining six chapters of the television series
‹Histoire(s) du cinéma›
_____ 1999 Éloge de l'amour (In Praise Of Love)
with Bruno Putzulu
_____ 2000 L'origine du XXIème siècle (Origin of the 21st Century)
documentary for the Cannes Film Festival, 2000

Selected Bibliography

_____ 1988 Godard on Godard
Critical Writings (Da Capo Press), by Jean-Luc Godard, Jean Narboni
(Editor), Tom Milne (Editor).
_____ 1999 The Films of Jean-Luc Godard
Seeing the Invisible (Cambridge Film Classics), by David Sterritt.

———— 1999 Histoire(s) du cinéma 1 – 4
(All the Stories – A Story Alone; The Cinema Alone – Fatal Beauty; La monnaie de l'absolu – A New Wave; Le contrôle de l'univers – The Signs Among Us), 4 volumes in English, French and German, with 5 CDs including the soundtrack, (ECM Records, Munich) by Jean-Luc Godard.
————2000 Jean-Luc Godard's Pierrot Le Fou
(Cambridge Film Handbooks), by David Wills.
————2001 The Cinema Alone
Jean-Luc Godard in the Year 2000 (Film Culture in Transition Series), by James S. Williams et al.

_____ Agee, James, 1909 – 1955

American author and screenwriter active in the forties; film critic for ‹Time› and ‹The Nation› (‹Agee On Film›, 1941, collected film critics). Collaborated with John Huston ‹The African Queen›, 1952.

_____ Anelka, Nicolas, b. 1979

French footballer and ‹enfant terrible›; has played for several teams including Paris St-Germain, Real Madrid, and Liverpool.

_____ Arendt, Hannah, 1906 – 1975

Sociologist/political scientist, American with German origins.

_____ Assayas, Olivier, b. 1955

Screenplay assistant with Téchiné (‹Rendez-vous›, 1985); later became a film director, influenced by Téchiné and Truffaut (‹Paris s'éveille›, 1991; ‹Les destinées sentimentales›, 2000).

_____ Aurenche, Jean, b. 1903

French screenwriter, worked for thirty years with Pierre Bost. Aurenche and Bost wrote a script about Bernanos' work, ‹Le journal d'un curé de campagne›, which was not accepted by him. After Bernanos' death in 1951, Robert Bresson made a film about the book using his own script.

_____ Auriol, Jean-Georges, 1907 – 1950

French critic who founded the magazine ‹Du cinéma› (subsequently to become ‹Revue du cinéma›) in 1928; it ran for 29 issues. In 1946 Auriol relaunched the magazine and it continued to run until after his death.

_____ Bardèche, Maurice, 1908 – 1998

French author, who wrote in 1935, together with his brother-in-law

Robert Brasillach, ‹Histoire du cinéma›, a very considered work which in many ways, especially in its anti-Semitism, is very dubious, but which is seen as a pioneer because of the universality of its claims.

_____ Bataille, Georges, 1897–1962

French essayist and philosopher who examined psychoanalysis, mystic, theological and ethnological questions. The text ‹Le bleu du ciel› was written in 1935, but published only 22 years later (‹Abbé C.›, 1950; ‹Le bleu du ciel›, 1957).

_____ Bazin, André, 1918–1958

French critic, co-founder in 1951 of ‹Cahiers du cinéma›, which he edited until his death. Is often called ‹father of the New Wave›.

_____ Becker, Jacques, 1906–1960

French film director (‹Grand Illusion›, 1937).

_____ Benigni, Roberto, b. 1952

Italian actor and director (actor in ‹Down by Law›, 1986; ‹Night on Earth›, 1991, for Jim Jarmusch; director of ‹La vita è bella› [‹Life is Beautiful›], 1997).

_____ Bergman, Ingmar, b. 1918

Swedish film and theater director (‹Das Schweigen› [‹The Silence›], 1963).

_____ Bernanos, Georges, 1888–1948

French Catholic writer (‹La joie›, 1929; ‹Le journal d'un curé de campagne›, 1936).

_____ Bernard, Marcel, b. 1914

French tennis player who won the first tennis contest in the Roland-Garros stadium in 1946.

_____ Bertolucci, Bernardo, b. 1941

Italian director, (‹Last Tango in Paris›, 1972; ‹The Last Emperor›, 1987; ‹Stealing Beauty›, 1996).

_____ Bettelheim, Bruno, 1903 – 1990

Important American psychologist, pioneer in the research of the infantile psyche, especially infantile autism (‹The Empty Fortress: Infantile Autism and the Birth of the Self›, 1967).

_____ Bitsch, Charles

Director's assistant to Godard (‹Breathless›, 1963; ‹Contempt›, 1963; ‹Deux ou trois choses que je sais d'elle›, 1966), author of short movies, film critic (‹Cahiers du cinéma›), TV-director.

_____ Blier, Bertrand b. 1939

French director whose movies contain black humor and surrealist elements (‹Les valseuses›, 1974; ‹Tenue de soirée›, 1986; ‹Les acteurs›, 2000).

_____ Boetsch, Arnaud, b. 1969

French tennis player who won the Davis Cup in 1991 and 1996 with the French team.

_____ Bory, Jean-Louis, 1919 – 1979

French writer and defender of the art of film; wrote for ‹Arts› (1961-1966) and ‹Le nouvel observateur› (1966-1979).

_____ Brasillach, Robert, 1909 – 1945

French author and journalist, who wrote ‹Histoire du cinéma›, with Maurice Bardèche. Executed in 1945 for collaboration with the Nazis.

_____ Braunberger, Pierre, 1905 – 1990

French producer and distributor, produced films by directors including Jean Renoir, Max Ophüls, François Truffaut and J.-L. Godard.

_____ Bresson, Robert, 1901 – 1999

French director (‹Pickpocket›, 1959); his ‹Notes sur le cinématographe› are often quoted by JLG.

_____ Campion, Jane, b. 1954

Australian director (‹An Angel at my Table›, 1990; ‹The Piano›, 1993).

_____ Capra, Frank, 1897 – 1991

American director of Italian origin (‹Arsenic and Old Laces›, 1943)

_____ Capriati, Jennifer, b. 1976

American tennis player.

_____ Carette, Julien, 1897 – 1966

French actor (‹La grande illusion› by Jean Renoir, 1937; ‹Adieu Leonard› by Pierre Prevert, 1943); acted in several comedies.

_____ Cassavetes, John, 1929 – 1989

American actor and director (‹Faces›, 1968; ‹Big Trouble›, 1987).

_____ Chaplin, Charles, 1889-1977

British actor, screenwriter and producer.

_____ Cioran, Emile, 1911 – 1995

Writer and philosopher, French with Rumanian origins.

_____ Coen, Joel, b. 1955, and Ethan, b. 1957

American directors (‹Fargo›, 1996; ‹The Big Lebowski›, 1998; ‹O Brother, Where Are Thou?› 2000).

_____ Constantine, Eddie, 1917 – 1993

American born international actor and singer (TV-series, detective-movies as Lemmy Caution, in different films for JLG (‹Contempt›, 1963; ‹Allemagne année 90 neuf zéro› [‹Germany Year 90›], 1991, and R.W. Fassbinder).

_____ Coppola, Francis Ford, b. 1939

American director, and Oscar-winner (‹The Godfather›, 1972; ‹Apocalypse Now›, 1979; ‹The Cotton Club›, 1984).

_____ Courier, Jim, b. 1970

American tennis player, achieved his greatest successes in the early nineties.

_____ Cournot, Michel

French film critic (‹Le nouvel observateur›, and later ‹Le monde›), film director (‹Les Gauloises bleues›, 1967) and author (‹Ossip Mandelstam›, 2000, a theater play).

89

——————— Cukor, George, 1899 – 1983
American director (‹My Fair Lady›, 1963).

——————— Cuny, Alain, 1908 – 1994
French actor (‹La dolce vita›, 1960; ‹Satyricon›, 1969, by Fellini).

——————— Daney, Serge, 1944 – 1992
French film critic working from 1965 at ‹Cahiers du cinéma› (1973-1981 as editor-in-chief), and subsequently at the daily ‹Libération›.

——————— De Sica, Vittorio, 1902 – 1974
Italian actor and director (‹The Bicycle Thief›, 1948; ‹Umberto D.›, 1952; ‹The Garden of the Finzi-Contini›, 1971).

——————— de Rougemont, Denis, 1906 – 1985
French-writing Swiss author and cultural philosopher.

——————— Delannoy, Jean, b. 1908
French director whose early films show strength and energy, but whose work from the forties onwards is mainly indifferent and arbitrary.

——————— Delluc, Louis, 1890 – 1924
French director, said to be one of the first French film critics. The French film prize ‹Prix Louis Delluc› is named after him.

——————— Desplechin, Arnaud, b. 1960
French director (‹La vie des morts›, 1991; ‹La sentinelle›, 1992; ‹Esther Kahn›, 2000).

——————— Douchet, Jean, b. 1929
Film critic and historian, called ‹the Socrates of the cinema›, wrote several books (‹La nouvelle vague – Jean-Luc Godard, François Truffaut, Claude Chabrol, Eric Rohmer›, 1998), closely connected to the New Wave, teaches at the Fémis.

——————— Duncan, Mary, 1895 – 1993
American actress in silent movies of the twenties and thirties, ‹films noir›, leading character in ‹The River› (1928) by Frank Borzage, and ‹City Girl› (1930) by F.M. Murnau; ceased acting in movies after 1930.

_____ Duras, Marguerite, 1914–1996

French writer (‹L'amant› [‹The Lover›], 1984), screenwriter (‹Hiroshima mon amour›, 1959) and director (‹India Song›, 1975).

_____ Duthu, Hervé

Sports commentator for Eurosport, often for tennis matches together with Arnaud Boetsch.

_____ Eisenschitz, Bernard

Translator of films and books, wrote many books about cinema, member of the editorial staff of the ‹Cinémathèque›, film journalist for ‹Cahiers du cinéma›.

_____ Fangio, Juan Manuel, 1911–1995

Argentinian racing motorist, last raced at the ‹Grand Prix de France› in 1958.

_____ Faure, Elie, 1873–1937

French philosopher, historian and art historian, one of the first intellectuals to look at the cinema as art.

_____ Fémis, La

‹Ecole nationale supérieure des métiers de l'image et du son›, French film academy in Paris, founded in 1984.

_____ Ferrara, Abel, b. 1952

American director of thrillers (‹King of New York›, 1989), Science fiction (‹Body Snatchers›, 1993) and Mafia films (‹The Funeral›, 1996).

_____ Ferré, Léo, 1916–1993

French author, composer and singer of poetic chansons; arranged works by poets such as Aragon, Apollinaire and Rimbaud.

_____ Ford, John, 1895–1973

American director of Irish origin, (‹My Darling Clementine›, 1946; ‹The Man Who Shot Liberty Valance›, 1962).

_____ Fresnoy, Le

‹Studio national des arts contemporains›, French center for the formation, research, and production in all fields of picture and sound.

_____ Frodon, Jean-Michel

Film critic at ‹Le monde›, author of various books about film; described ‹Éloge de l'amour› as a «work full of beauty and spirit, a stroll accompanied by assonances and harmonies».

_____ Fuller, Samuel, 1911 – 1997

American director of war films (‹Steel Helmet›, 1951; ‹The Big Red One›, 1979), his work is considered controversial; makes a brief appearance in J-L. Godard's ‹Pierrot le fou›.

_____ Gallo, Max, b. 1932

Historian, author, essayist, leftwing intellectual, published a biography of Napoleon in 1997.

_____ Giraudoux, Jean, 1882 – 1944

French author (‹Eglantine›, 1927 [novel]; ‹The Madwoman of Chaillot›, 1945 [play]).

_____ Goupil, Romain, b. 1951

French director (‹Mourir à trente ans›, 1982; ‹À mort la mort›, 1999, in which he also acted).

_____ Green, Julien, 1900 – 1998

French author of American origin.

_____ Griffith, D.W., 1875 – 1948

Legendary American director (‹Birth of a Nation›, 1915; ‹Broken Blossoms›, 1919).

_____ Guiguet, Jean-Claude, b. 1943

French director (‹Le mirage›, 1992, after Thomas Mann's novel ‹Der Erwählte›); showed ‹Les passagers› at the Cannes Film Festival in 1999.

_____ Halberstadt, Michèle

French producer, produced ‹Éloge de l'amour›.

_____ Hawks, Howard, 1896 – 1977

American director (‹Scarface›, 1932).

_____ Hitchcock, Alfred, 1899 – 1980

American director (‹Vertigo›, 1958).

_____ Hollande, François, b. 1954

French politician, succeeded Lionel Jospin as General Secretary of the Socialist party in 1977.

_____ Holt, Jany, b. 1912

French actress of Rumanian origin (‹Bas-fonds› [‹The Lower Depths›] by Jean Renoir, 1937; ‹Les anges du péché› [‹Angels of the Streets›] by Robert Bresson, 1943).

_____ Huston, John, 1906–1987

American director (‹The Maltese Falcon›, 1941; ‹The African Queen› 1952; ‹The Misfits›, 1960; ‹Chinatown›, 1974).

_____ Ishaghpour, Youssef

French film critic and author, writings include ‹Orson Welles cinéaste, une caméra visible› and, together and in conversation with Godard, ‹Archéologie du cinéma et mémoire du siècle›, 2000.

_____ Jacob, Gilles, b. 1930

President of the Cannes Film Festival for over twenty years (until 2000).

_____ ‹Kapo›, 1959

French-Italian co-production by Gillo Pontecorvo with Susan Strasberg, Laurent Terzieff and Emmanuelle Riva, about a woman who is taken prisoner by the Nazis.

_____ Kazan, Elia, b. 1909

American director and screenwriter (‹Viva Zapata›, 1951; ‹East of Eden›, 1955; ‹The Last Tycoon›, 1976).

_____ Kubrick, Stanley, b. 1928

American director (‹Clockwork orange›, 1971; ‹The Shining›, 1980; ‹Eyes Wide Shut›, 1999).

_____ Kurnikowa, Anna, b. 1981

Russian tennis player.

_____ Lang, Fritz, 1890–1976

American director, screenwriter and producer of Austrian origin;

actor in ‹Contempt› by JLG (‹Metropolis›, 1926; ‹M›, 1931; ‹The Thousand Eyes of Dr. Mabuse›, 1960).

————— Langlois, Henri, 1914–1977

Co-founder and General secretary of ‹Cinémathèque française›.

————— Lelouch, Claude, b. 1937

French director, screenwriter and producer (‹Un homme et une femme› [‹A Man and a Woman›], 1966; ‹Toute une vie› [‹Live for Life›], 1984; ‹Les misérables›, 1994).

————— Lévinas, Emmanuel, 1905–1995

French philosopher, influenced by Husserl and Heidegger.

————— Lucas, George, b. 1933

American director of films including the ‹Star Wars› series.

————— Lumière, Auguste, 1862–1954

French photography pioneer; constructed the first cinematograph with his brother Louis in 1894.

————— Mac Laren, Norman, 1914–1987

Canadian experimental filmmaker of Scottish origin, who perfected the technique of painting images to be animated directly on the film stock.

————— Makhmalbaf, Mohsen, b. 1951

Iranian director, imprisoned during the Shah's regime (1974 – 1979) (‹Boycott›, 1985; ‹Salaam Cinema›, 1993; ‹Kandahar›, 2001). Father of filmmaker Samira Makhmalbaf, (‹La Pomme› [‹The Apple›], 1997; ‹Blackboards›, 2000).

————— Malraux, André, 1901–1976

French writer, director and politician (‹L'espoir›, a novel about the Spanish civil war (1937), was filmed by Malraux in 1939 [‹A Man's Hope›]).

————— Marceau, Sophie, b. 1966

French actress (‹La boum›, 1980; ‹Braveheart›, 1995; ‹Anna Karenina›, 1997; ‹The World is not Enough›, 1999).

_____ McEnroe, John Patrick, b. 1959

American tennis player, successful in the eighties.

_____ Mecir, Miroslav, b. 1964

Czech tennis player, Olympia winner in 1988.

_____ Méliès, Georges, 1861–1938

French film pioneer, discovered film as a public entertainment in 1896.

_____ Miéville, Anne-Marie, b. 1945

Swiss director, has worked since 1972 in collaboration with J.-L. Godard, and on her own movies (‹Mon cher sujet› [‹My Dear Subject›], 1988; ‹Nous sommes tous encore ici› [‹We're All Still Here›], 1997).

_____ Miller, Claude, b. 1942

French director, mentored by Godard and Truffaut (‹Garde à vue› [‹Under Suspicion›], 1981; ‹La petite voleuse› [‹The Little Thief›], 1988; ‹La chambre des magiciennes› [‹Of Women and Magic›], 2001, with video techniques).

_____ Novak, Kim, b. 1933

American actress, active from the fifties to the seventies (‹Vertigo›, 1958, by Alfred Hitchcock).

_____ Ostermeyer, Micheline, 1923–2001

French athletic and pianist, won first price at the Music Academy in Paris in 1946, and in 1948 was a triple Olympia winner in London; active as a concert pianist from 1950.

_____ Palance, Jack, b. 1919

American actor (‹Contempt›, by JLG).

_____ Péguy, Charles, 1873–1914

French author and editor (‹Cahiers de la quinzaine›). ‹Clio, dialogue de l'histoire et de l'âme païenne› was published in 1909.

_____ Puskas, Czibor, Hidegkuti

Hungarian football champions in the fifties.

_____ Putzulu, Bruno, b. 1967

French actor; acted in ‹Les passagers› (1998) by Jean-Claude Guiguet and on the strength of the role was engaged by Godard for ‹Éloge de l'amour›.

_____ Ray, Nicolas, 1911–1979

American director, friend of Elia Kazan, (‹They Live by Night›, 1949; ‹Rebel Without a Cause›, 1955).

_____ Renoir, Jean, 1894–1979

French director and screen play writer (‹Madame Bovary›, 1934).

_____ Rivette, Jacques, b. 1928

French film critic and director, founded, together with Truffaut, Godard and Rohmer, ‹Gazette du cinéma› in 1950, which ran for only five issues. From 1953 onwards, he worked at ‹Cahiers du cinéma›, (1963-1965 as editor-in-chief). Films include ‹Paris nous appartient›, 1961; ‹La religieuse›, 1966; ‹Céline et Julie vont en bateau›, 1974; ‹Jeanne la pucelle› [‹Joan the Maid›], 1994.

_____ Rocha, Glauber, 1938–1981

Brazilian director and member of the ‹Cinema Novo› movement in the 1960s in Brazil (‹Black God, White Devil›, 1964; ‹Land in a Trance›, 1967; ‹Antonio das Mortas›, 1969).

_____ Rohmer, Eric, b. 1920

French film critic and director, editor of ‹Cahiers du cinéma› 1958-63 (‹Bérénice›, 1974 (short movie); ‹Ma nuit chez Maude›, 1969; ‹L'anglaise et le duc›, 2001).

_____ Roland-Garros

Tennis court in Paris, named after the French pilot Roland Garros (1882-1918), who was the first Frenchman to fly across the Mediterranean.

_____ Rosselini, Roberto, 1906–1977

Italian director, representative of Neo-realism (‹Roma – città aperta› [‹Rome, Open City›], 1945; ‹Voyage in Italy›, 1953).

———————— Rostand, Jean, 1894 – 1977

French biologist and author, researcher on teratology (deformities) of frogs and toads; famous for his popular scientific writings and moral-philosophical reflections.

———————— Rouch, Jean, b. 1917

French director, representative of ‹Cinéma vérité›, made many films in Africa (‹Moi, un noir› [‹I a Negro›], 1958; ‹Enigma›, 1988; ‹Moi fatigué debout, moi couché› [‹I Am Tired of Standing, I Lie Down›], 1997).

———————— Rouquier, Georges, 1909 – 1989

French director (‹Farrebique›, 1946; ‹Sangre y luces›, 1954; ‹Biquefarre›, 1984).

———————— Sarde, Alain

French producer. Films include ‹Sauve qui peut (la vie)› and ‹Prénom Carmen› by Godard.

———————— Séguret, Olivier

Film critic at ‹Libération›, called Godard's film ‹Éloge de l'amour› his lyric confession.

———————— Senna, Ayrton, 1960 – 1994

Brazilian car-racer, died in an accident in Imola at the Grand Prix of San Marino.

———————— Snow, Michael, b. 1929

American experimental filmmaker active since 1963 (‹Wavelength›, 1967; ‹La région centrale›, 1971).

———————— Sotomayor, Javier, b. 1967

Cuban high jumper, first to exceed 8 feet, gold medal (1992), silver medal (2000) at the Olympics.

———————— Stevens, George, 1904 – 1975

American director, (‹Swing Time›, 1936). ‹A Place in the Sun› (1951), with Elisabeth Taylor and Montgomery Clift, won an Oscar and is one of the key movies of the fifties.

———————— Straub, Jean-Marie, b. 1933

First assistant to Jean Renoir and Robert Bresson; became a director in 1958. Works with his partner Danièle Huillet (‹Sicilia›, 1999).

————— Szabo, Gabriela, b. 1976

Rumanian middle-distance runner, Olympic winner in 1996, 2000.

————— Taris, Jean

French swimming champion in the thirties, Jean Vigo made a documentary about him (‹La natation›, 1931).

————— Téchiné, André b. 1943

French director (‹Rendez-vous›, 1985; ‹Les roseaux sauvages›, 1994; ‹Loin›, 2001).

————— Truffaut, François, 1932–1984

French director, protagonist of the New Wave (‹Jules et Jim›, 1961; ‹Le dernier métro›, 1980). Wrote the article ‹A Certain Tendency in French Cinema›, in ‹Cahiers du cinéma› (1951) in which he attacked and criticized Aurenche's and Bost's screenplay for ‹Le journal d'un curé de campagne›.

————— Ulmer, Edgar, 1900–1972

Independent American director with Austrian origins, known as the ‹King of the B-movies› (‹Bluebeard›, 1944; ‹The Naked Dawn›, 1955).

————— Verny, Françoise

Editor at Gallimard, later at Flammarion, made films of literary works for TV, plays the role of the grandmother in ‹Éloge de l'amour›.

————— Vidor, King W., 1894–1982

American director (‹Duel in the Sun›, 1946; ‹War and Peace›, 1956; ‹Solomon and Sheba›, 1959).

————— Vigo, Jean, 1905–1934

French director (‹A propos de Nice›, 1929; ‹La Natation›, 1931; ‹Zéro de conduite›, 1933; ‹L'atalante›, 1934), had great influence on surrealist films and New Wave; admired by JLG.

————— Vinterberg, Thomas

Danish director (‹Celebration›, 1998, after the rules of the Scandinavian group ‹Dogma 95›).

————— Visconti, Luchino, 1906–1976

Italian director (‹The Leopard›, 1963; ‹Death in Venice›, 1971).

_____ von Sydow, Max, b. 1929

Swedish actor in films by Bergman among others.

_____ von Trier, Lars

Danish director (‹Idiots›, 1998, after the rules of the Scandinavian group ‹Dogma 95›).

_____ Warhol, Andy, 1927–1987

American artist and filmmaker.

_____ Welles, Orson, 1915–1985

American actor and director (‹The Lady from Shanghai› 1948; ‹Touch of Evil›, 1958; ‹F for Fake›, 1975).

_____ Williams, Venus, b. 1980

American tennis player.

Mr Whistler's Ten O'Clock
Public lecture, Prince's Hall, Piccadilly, 20 February 1885

Ladies and Gentlemen!

It is with great hesitation and much misgiving that I appear before you, in the character of – The Preacher.

If timidity be at all allied to the virtue modesty, and can find favor in your eyes, I pray you, for the sake of that virtue, accord me your utmost indulgence.

I would plead for my want of habit, did it not seem preposterous, judging from precedent, that aught save the most efficient effrontery, could be ever expected in connection with my subject – for I will not conceal from you, that I mean to talk about Art! Yes, Art – that has, of late become, as far as much discussion and writing can make it, a sort of common topic for the Tea table.

Art is upon the Town! – to be chucked under the chin, by the passing gallant! – to be enticed within the gates of the householder – to be coaxed into company, as a proof of culture and refinement!

If familliarity can breed contempt, certainly Art, or what is currently taken for it, has been brought to its lowest stage of intimacy!

The people have been harrassed with Art in every guise – and vexed with many methods, as to its endurance – They have been told how they shall love Art! and live with it – Their homes have been invaded – their walls covered with paper – their very dress taken to task, – until roused at last, bewildered and filled with the doubts and discomforts of senseless suggestion, they resent such intrusion, and cast forth the false prophets, who have brought the very name of the beautiful into disrepute, – and derision upon themselves.

Alas! ladies and gentlemen – Art has been maligned – she has nought in common with such practices – She is a goddess of dainty thought – reticent of habit – abjuring all obtrusiveness – proposing in no way to better others.

She is withal selfishly occupied with her own perfection only – having no desire to teach – seeking and finding the beautiful in all conditions, and in all times – As did her high priest Rembrandt, when he saw picturesque grandeur and noble dignity in the Jews' quarter of Amsterdam – and lamented not that its inhabitants were not Greeks.

As did Tintoret and Paul Veronese, among the Venetians – while not halting to change the brocaded silks for the classic draperies of Athens.

As did, at the Court of Philip, Velasquez, whose Infantas clad in inaesthetic hoops, are, as works of Art, of the same quality as the Elgin marbles.

No reformers were these great men – no improvers of the ways of others! – Their productions, alone, were their occupation, and, filled with the poetry of their science, they required not to alter their surroundings – for as the laws of their Art were revealed to them, they saw, in the developement of their work, that real beauty, which, to them, was as much a matter of certainty and triumph, as is to the astronomer, the verification of the result, foreseen, with the light given to him alone. – In all this, their world was completely severed from that of their fellow creatures, with whom, sentiment is mistaken for poetry, and for whom, there is no perfect work, that shall not be explained by the benefit conferred upon themselves – Humanity takes the place of Art – and God's creations are excused by their usefulness. Beauty is confounded with Virtue, and, before a work of Art, it is asked: «What good shall it do?»

Hence it is that nobility of action, in this life, is hopelessly linked with the merit of the work that portrays it – and thus the people have acquired the habit of looking, as who should say, not at a picture, but ‹through› it, at some human fact, that shall, or shall not, from a social point of view, better their mental, or moral state – So we have come to hear of the painting that elevates, – and of the duty of the painter – of the picture that is full of thought – and of the panel that merely decorates.

A favorite faith, dear to those who teach, is that certain periods were especially artistic, and that nations, readily named, were notably lovers of Art.

So we are told that the Greeks were, as a people, worshippers of the beautiful, and that in the fifteenth century, Art was engrained in the multitude.

That the great masters lived, in common understanding with their patrons – that the early Italians were artists – all! – and that the demand for the lovely thing, produced it.

That we of today, in gross contrast to this Arcadian purity, call for the ungainly, and obtain the ugly.

That could we but change our habits and climate – were we willing to wander in groves – could we be roasted out of broadcloth, were we to do without haste, and journey without speed, we should again ‹require› the spoon of Queen Anne, and pick at our peas with the fork of two prongs! And so, for the flock, little hamlets grow, near Hammersmith, and the steam horse is scorned.

Useless! quite hopeless and false is the effort! – built upon fable, and all because «a wise man has uttered a vain thing and filled his belly with the East wind.»

Listen! – there ‹never› was an artistic period!

There never was an art loving nation.

In the beginning, man went forth each day – some to do battle – some to the chase – others again to dig and to delve in the field – all that they might gain, and live – or lose and die – until there was found among them, one, differing from the rest – whose pursuits attracted him not – and so he staid by the tents, with the women, and traced strange devices, with a burnt stick, upon a gourd.

This man, who took no joy in the ways of his brethren, who cared not for conquest, and fretted in the field – this designer of quaint patterns – this deviser of the beautiful, who perceived in nature about him, curious curvings, – as faces are seen in the fire – This dreamer apart – was the ‹first› artist.

And when, from the field and from afar, there came back the people, they took the gourd and drank from out of it.

And presently there came to this man another – and, in time others – of like nature – chosen by the Gods – and so they worked together – and soon they fashioned, from the moistened earth, forms resembling the gourd – and, with the power of creation, the heirloom of the artist, presently they went beyond the slovenly suggestion of Nature – and the first vase was born, in beautiful proportion.

And the toilers tilled, and were athirst, – and the heroes returned from fresh victories, to rejoice and to feast – and all drank alike from the Artists goblets, fashioned cunningly – taking no note the while of the craftsman's pride and understanding not his glory in his work – drinking, at the cup, not from choice, not from a consciousness that it was beautiful – but because, forsooth, there was none other!

And time, with more state, brought more capacity for luxury, and it became well that men should dwell in large houses and rest upon couches, and eat at tables – whereupon the artist, with his artificers, built palaces, and filled them with furniture, beautiful in proportion, and lovely to look upon.

And the people lived in marvels of Art – and eat and drank out of Masterpieces – for there was nothing else to eat and to drink out of – and no bad building to live in – no article of daily life – of luxury, or of necessity that had not been handed down from the design of the Master, and made by his workmen.

And the people questioned not – and had nothing to say in the matter.

So Greece was in its splendour – and Art reigned supreme – by force of fact – not by election – and there was no muddling from the outsider – The mighty warrior would no more have ventured to offer a design for the temple of Pallas Athene, than would the ‹sacred› poet have proffered a plan for constructing the catapult.

And the Amateur was unknown – and the Dilettante undreamed of.

And history wrote on – and conquest accompanied civilisation – and Art spread – or rather its products were carried by the victors among the vanquished from one country to another – And the customs of cultivation covered the face of the earth – so that all peoples continued to use what ‹the artist alone produced›.

And centuries passed in this using, and the world was flooded with all that was beautiful – until there arose a new class who discovered the cheap – and foresaw fortune in the facture of the sham.

Then sprang into existence, the tawdry – the common – the gewgaw.

The ‹taste› of the tradesman, supplanted the ‹science› of the artist – and what was born of the million, went back to them –

106

and charmed them – for it was after their own heart – and the great and the small, the statesman and the slave, took to themselves the abomination that was tendered, and preferred it, and have lived with it ever since.

And the Artists occupation was gone – and the manufacurer and the huckster took his place.

And now the heroes filled from the jugs, and drank from the bowls, with understanding – noting the glare of their new bravery, and taking pride in its worth.

And the people, this time, had much to say in the matter – and all were satisfied – and Birmingham and Manchester arose in their might, and Art was relegated to the curiosity shop.

Nature contains the elements of color and form of all pictures – as the keyboard contains the notes of all music.

But the artist is born to pick, and choose, and group with science, these elements, that the result may be beautiful – as the musician gathers his notes, and forms his chords, until he brings forth from chaos, glorious harmony.

To say to the painter, that nature is to be taken, as she is, is to say to the player, that he may sit on the piano!

That Nature is always right, is an assertion, artistically, as untrue, as it is one whose truth is universally taken for granted – Nature is very rarely right, to such an extent even, that it might almost be said that Nature is usually wrong – that is to say – the condition of things that shall bring about the perfection of harmony worthy a picture, is rare, and not common at all.

This would seem, to even the most intelligent, a doctrine almost blasphemous – So incorporated with our education has the supposed aphorism become, that its belief is held to be part of our moral being – and the words themselves have, in our ear, the ring of religion! – Still, seldom does nature succeed in producing a picture.

The sun blares – and the wind blows from the East – the sky is bereft of cloud – and without, all is made of iron – The windows of the Crystal Palace are seen from all points of London – the holiday maker rejoices in the glorious day – and the painter turns aside to shut his eyes.

How little this is understood, and how dutifully the casual in Nature, is accepted as sublime, may be gathered from the unlimited admiration, daily produced, by a very foolish sunset.

The dignity of the snowcapped mountain is lost in distinctness – but the joy of the tourist is to recognise the traveller on the top – The desire to see, for the sake of seeing, is, with the mass, alone the one to be gratified – hence the delight in detail – and when the evening mist clothes the riverside with poetry, as with a veil – and the poor buildings lose themselves in the dim sky – and the tall chimneys become campanile – and the warehouses are palaces in the night – and the whole city hangs in the heavens, and faireyland is before us – then the wayfarer hastens home – the working man and the cultured one – the wise man and the one of pleasure – cease to understand, as they have ceased to see – and Nature, who for once, has sung in tune, sings her exquisite song to the Artist alone, her son and her master – her son in that he loves her, her master in that he knows her.

To him her secrets are unfolded – to him her lessons have become gradually clear – He looks at her flower, not with the enlarging lens, that he may gather facts for the botanist, but, with the light of the one, who sees, in her choice selection of brilliant tones and delicate tints, suggestions of future harmonies.

He does not confine himself to purposeless copying, without thought, each blade of grass, as commended by the inconsequent – but, in the long curve of the narrow leaf, corrected by the straight tall stem, he learns how grace is wedded to dignity, how strength enhances sweetness, that elegance shall be the result.

In the citron wing of the pale butterfly with its dainty spots of orange – he sees before him the stately halls of fair gold, with their slender safron pillars – and is taught how the delicate drawing, high upon the walls, shall be traced in tender tones of orpiment, and repeated by the base, in notes of graver hue.

In all that is dainty, and loveable, he finds hints for his own combinations, and thus is Nature ever his resource – and always at his service – and to him is naught refused.

Through his brain, as through the last alembic, is distilled the refined escence of that thought which began with the Gods, and which they left him to carry out.

Set apart by them to complete their works, he produces that wondrous thing called the masterpiece, which surpasses in perfection, all that they have contrived in what is called Nature, and the Gods stand by, and marvel – and perceive how far away more beautiful is the Venus of Melos, than was their own Eve.

For some time past the unattached writer has become the middleman in this matter of Art – and his influence, while it has widened the gulf between the people and the painter, has brought about the most complete misunderstanding as to the aim of the picture.

For him, a picture is more or less a hieroglyph or symbol of story – Apart from a few technical terms, for the display of which he finds an occasion, the work is considered absolutely from a literarypoint of view – indeed from what other can he consider it – and in his essays he deals with it, as with a novel, a history or an anecdote.

He fails entirely, and most naturally to see its excellencies, or demerits, artistic, and so degrades Art – as supposing it a method of bringing about a literary climax.

It thus, in his hands, becomes mainly a method of perpetrating something further, and its mission is made a secondary one, even as a means is second to an end.

The thoughts emphasized, noble or other, are inevitably attached to the incident – and become more or less noble, according to the eloquence or mental quality of the writer, who looks, the while, with disdain, upon what he holds as ‹mere execution› – a matter belonging, he believes, to the training of the schools, and the reward of assiduity – So that as he goes on, with his translation, from canvas to paper, the work becomes his own – He finds poetry, where he would feel it, were he himself transcribing the event – invention, in the intricacy of the mise en scène – and noble philosophy in some detail of philanthropy – courage, modesty, or virtue sugested to him by the occurrence.

All this might be brought before him and appeal to his imagination, by a very poor picture – indeed I might safely say that it generally is.

Meanwhile, the painter's poetry, is quite lost to him – The amazing invention that shall have put form and color into such perfect harmony that exquisiteness is the result, is without understanding – the nobility of thought that shall have given the artist's dignity to the whole, says to him absolutely nothing.

So that his praises are published, for virtues we would blush to possess – while the great qualities that distinguish the one work from the thousand, that make of the masterpiece the thing of beauty that it is, – have never been seen at all.

That this is so, we can make sure of by looking back at old Reviews upon past Exhibitions, and reading the flatteries lavished upon men who have since been forgotten altogether, – but upon whose works the language has been exhausted in rhapsodies that left nothing for the National Gallery!

A curious matter in its effect upon the judgement of these gentlemen, is the accepted vocabulary of poetic symbolism that helps them by habit in dealing with nature – A mountain to them, is synonymous with height – a lake, with depth – the ocean with vastness – the sun with glory.

So that a picture with a mountain, a lake and an Ocean, however poor in paint, is inevitably lofty – vast – ‹infinite› and ‹glorious› on paper.

There are those also, sombre of mien, and wise with the wisdom of books, who frequent museums and burrow in crypts – Collecting – comparing – compiling – classifying – contradicting – Experts these – for whom a date is an accomplishment – a hall-mark, success – Careful in scrutiny, are they, and conscientious of judgement – Establishing, with due weight, ... unimportant reputations – discovering the picture, by the stain on the back – testing the Torso, by the leg that is missing – filling folios with doubts on the way of that limb – disputatious and dictatorial, concerning the birthplace ... of inferior persons – speculating ... in much writing, upon the great worth of bad work – ... True clerks of the collection, they mix memoranda with ambition – and reducing Art to Statistics, they ‹file› the Fifteenth Century and pigeonhole the Antique!

Then the ‹Preacher› – appointed! – He stands in high places – harangues and holds forth – Sage of the Universities – learned in many matters, and of much experience in all save his subject.

Exhorting – denouncing – directing.

Filled with worth and Earnestness.

Bringing powers of persuasion and polish of language to prove – nothing!

Torn with much teaching – having naught to impart.

Impressive – important – shallow.

Defiant – distressed – desperate – crying out, and cutting himself while the Gods hear not gentle-priest of the Philistine, withal, again he ambles pleasantly from all point, and, through many volumes, escaping scientific assertion, ‹babbles of green fields›.

So Art has become foolishly confounded with education – that all should be equally qualified.

Whereas, while polish, refinement, culture and breeding, are, in no way, arguements for artistic result, it is also no reproach to the most finished scholar or greatest gentleman in the land that he be absolutely without eye for painting, or ear for music – that in his heart he prefer the popular print to the scratch of Rembrandts needle – or the songs of the Hall to Beethovens ‹C minor Symphony›.

if he have but the wit to say so – and do not feel the admission a proof of inferiority.

Art happens – no hovel is safe from it – no Prince may depend upon it – the vastest intelligence cannot bring it about – and puny efforts to make it universal end in quaint comedy – and coarse farce.

This is as it should be – and all attempts to make it otherwise are due to the eloquence of the ignorant – the zeal of the conceited – The boundary line is clear – Far from me to propose to bridge it over, that the pestered people be pushed across.

No! I would save them from further fatigue – I would come to their relief, and would lift from their shoulders this incubus of Art!

Why, after centuries of freedom from it, and indifference to it, should it now be thrust upon them by the blind! – until wearied and puzzled they know no longer how they shall eat or drink – how they shall sit or stand – or wherewithal they shall clothe themselves – without afflicting Art!

But lo! there is much talk without!

Triumphantly they cry ‹Beware›! – This matter does indeed concern art! – We also have our part in all true Art! – for remember the «one touch of Nature», that, «makes the whole world kin!»

True indeed – but let not the unwary jauntily suppose that Shakespeare herewith hands ‹him›, his passport to Paradise – and thus permits him speech among the chosen – Rather learn that, in this very sentence, he is condemned to remain without – to continue with the common.

This one chord that vibrates with all – this «one touch of nature» that calls aloud to the response of each – that explains the popularity of the Bull of Paul Potter.

that excuses the price of Murillo’s Conception – this one unspoken sympathy that pervades humanity – is Vulgarity!

Vulgarity – under whose facinating influence ‹the many› have elbowed ‹the few› – and the gentle circle of Art swarms with the intoxicated mob of mediocrity, whose leaders prate and council, and call aloud, where the Gods once spoke in whisper!

And now from their midst the Dilettante stalks abroad! – The Amateur is loosed – the voice of the Aesthete is heard in the land – and catastrophe is upon us!

The medler beckons the vengeance of the Gods – and ridicule threatens the fair daughters of the land.

For there are curious converts to a weird Culte, in which, all instinct for attractiveness – all freshness and sparkle – all woman's winsomeness, is to give way to a strange vocation for the unlovely! – and this desecration, in the name of the Graces!

Shall this gaunt, ill at ease – distressed – abashed mixture of mauvaise honte and desperate assertion, call itself artistic – and claim cousinship with the artist? – who delights in the dainty – the sharp bright gaiety of beauty!

No! a thousand times no! – Here are no connections of ours! We will have nothing to do with them.

Forced to seriousness, that emptiness may be hidden – they dare not smile.

While the artist, in fulness of heart and head, is glad and laughs aloud – and is happy in his strength – and is merry at the pompous pretention – the solemn silliness that surrounds him! –

For Art and Joy go together – with bold openess – and high head and ready hand – fearing naught – and dreading no exposure.

Know then all beautiful women, that we are with you – pay no heed we pray you to this outcry of the unbecoming – this last plea for the plain!

It concerns you not.

Your own instinct is near the truth – your own wit far surer guide than the untaught ventures of these thick headed Apollos!

What! will you come up and follow the first piper that leads you down Petticoat Lane, there, on a Sabbath, to gather, for the week, from the dull rags of Ages, wherewith to bedeck yourselves! – that beneath your travestied awkwardness, we have trouble to find your own dainty selves! Oh fi! – Is the world then exhausted! – and must we go back, because the thumb of the mountebank jerks the other way?

Costume is not dress.

and the wearers of wardrobes may not be doctors of 'taste'! – For by what authority shall these be pretty masters! – Look well, and nothing have they invented! – nothing put together for comeliness' sake.

Haphazard from their shoulders hang the garments of the Hawker – combining in their person, the motley of manny manners, with the medley of the mummers' closet.

Set up as a warning, and a fingerpost of danger – they point to the disastrous effect of Art upon the Middle Classes.

Why this lifting of the brow in deprecation of the present? – this pathos in reference to the past!

If Art be rare today, it was seldom heretofore.

It is false this teaching of decay.

The Master stands in no relation to the moment at which he occurs – a monument of isolation – hinting at sadness – having no part in the progress of his fellow men

He is also no more the product of civilisation than is the scientific truth asserted, dependent upon the wisdom of a period. – The assertion itself requires the ‹man› to make it – the truth was from the beginning.

So Art is limited to the infinite, and beginning there cannot progress.

A silent indication of its wayward independence from all extraneous advance, is the absolutely unchanged condition and form of implement, since the beginning of things.

The painter has but the same pencil – the sculptor the chisel of centuries.

Colours are not more since the heavy hangings of night were first drawn aside, and the loveliness of light revealed! Neither Chemist nor Engineer can offer new elements of the Masterpiece.

False again is the fabled link between the grandeur of Art, and the glories and virtues of the State – for Art feeds not upon Nations – and peoples may be wiped from the face of the Earth, but Art is.

It is indeed high time that we cast aside the weary weight of responsability and copartnership – and know that, in no way, do our virtues minister to its worth – in no way, do our vices impede its triumph!

How irksome! how hopeless! how superhuman the self imposed task of the Nation! – how sublimely vain the belief that it shall live nobly – or Art perish!

Let us reassure ourselves – at our own option, is our virtue – Art, we in no way affect.

A whimsical Goddess – and a capricious – her strong sense of joy tolerates no dulness – and live we never so spotlessly, still may she turn her back upon us.

As, from time immemorial, has she done upon the Swiss in their mountains.

What more worthy People! – whose every Alpine gap yawns with tradition, and is stocked with noble story – and yet the perverse and scornful one will none of it – and the sons of Patriots are left with the clock that turns the mill, or the sudden Cookoo, with difficulty restrained in its box.

For this was Tell a hero! – for this did Gessler die!

Art, the cruel jade cares not – and hardens her heart, and

hies her off to the East – to find, among the opium eaters of Nankin, a favorite with whom she lingers fondly – carressing his blue porcelain, and painting his coy maidens – and marking his plates with her six marks of choice – indifferent, in her companionship with him, to all save the virtue of his refinement!

‹He› it is who calls her – ‹he› who holds her.

And again to the West that her next lover may bring together the gallery at Madrid – and show the World how the Master towers above all – and in their intimacy they revel, he and she, in this knowledge – and he knows the happiness untasted by other mortel.

She is proud of her comrade – and promises that in after years others shall pass that way and understand.

So in all time does this superb one cast about for the man worthy her love – and Art seeks the Artist alone.

Where ‹he› is, there ‹she› appears – and remains with him – loving and fruitful – turning never aside in moments of hope deferred – of insult and of ribald misunderstanding.

and when he dies, she sadly takes her flight – though loitering yet in the land – from fond association – but refusing to be consoled.

And so have we the ephemeral influence of the Master's memory – the afterglow, in which are warmed, for awhile, the worker and disciple.

With the man, then, and not with the multitude are her intimacies – and in the book of her life, the names inscribed are few – scant indeed the list of those who have helped to write her story of love and beauty.

From the sunny morning, when, with her glorious Greek, relenting, she yielded up the secret of repeated line, as, with his hand in hers, together they marked, in marble, the measured rhyme of lovely limb, and draperies flowing in unison, to the day, when she dipped the Spaniard's brush in light and air, and made his people ‹live› within their frames, and ‹stand upon their legs› – that all no-bility, and sweetness, and tenderness, and magnificence should be theirs by right, ages had gone by, and ‹few› had been her choice!

Countless, indeed, the horde of pretenders! but she knew them not! – a teeming, seething, busy mass! – whose virtue was In-dustry – and whose Industry was vice.

Their names go to fill the catalogue of the Collection at home – of the Gallery Abroad – for the delectation of the bagman, and the Critic!

Therefore have we cause to be merry! – and to cast away all care – re-solved that all is well, as it ever was – and that it is not meet that we should be cried at, and urged to take measures.

Enough have we endured of dullness! – Surely are we weary of weeping – and our tears have been cozened from us falsely – for they have called out 'woe'! when there was no grief– and alas! where all is fair.

We have then but to wait – until, with the mark of the Gods upon him, there comes among us, again, the chosen, who shall con-tinue what has gone before – satisfied that even, were he never to ap-pear, the story of the beautiful is already complete – hewn in the marbles of the Parthenon, and broidered, with the birds, upon the fan of Hokusai – at the foot of Fusihama.

From the original manuscript in Glasgow University Library (Whistler W780): the transcription given here retains Whistler's spelling. The text was privately printed in 1885; minor revisons were made in 1886, and the lecture was finally published by Chatto and Windus in 1888.

119

Sources

_____ The Future(s) of Film

Translated from ‹Avenir(s) du cinéma, Entretien avec Jean-Luc Godard›, Cahiers du cinéma, special issue for the Cannes Film Festival, May 2000

_____ A Long Story

Translated from ‹Jean-Luc Godard – Une longue histoire›, Cahiers du cinema, No. 557, May 2001

_____ Movies Lie, Not Sports

Translated from ‹Le cinéma ment, pas le sport›, L'Equipe, May 9, 2001

_____ Mr. Whistler's Ten O'Clock

Original manuscript in Glasgow University Library (Whistler W780)

Copyright for the English edition

Verlag Gachnang & Springer AG, Bern 2002

homepage

www.gachnang-springer.com

Translations

John O'Toole, Catherine Schelbert

Language Editor

Rowena Joy Smith Robinson

Glossary and Production Coordinator

Constance Lotz

Editors

Christiane Meyer-Thoss and Constance Lotz

Design by

typoundso.ch

Printed and bound by

Victor Hotz AG, Steinhausen

Printed in Switzerland

ISBN 3-906127-62-1